Bridging UX and Web Development

T0383325

Bridging UX and Web Development

Better Results through Team Integration

Jack Moffett

AMSTERDAM • BOSTON • HEIDELBERG • LONDON
NEW YORK • OXFORD • PARIS • SAN DIEGO
SAN FRANCISCO • SINGAPORE • SYDNEY • TOKYO

Morgan Kaufmann is an imprint of Elsevier

Acquiring Editor: Meg Dunkerley
Editorial Project Manager: Lindsay Lawrence
Project Manager: Punithavathy Govindaradjane
Designer: Alan Studholme

Morgan Kaufmann is an imprint of Elsevier
225 Wyman Street, Waltham, MA, 02451, USA

Copyright © 2014 Elsevier Inc. All rights reserved.

No part of this publication may be reproduced or transmitted in any form or by any means, electronic or mechanical, including photocopying, recording, or any information storage and retrieval system, without permission in writing from the publisher. Details on how to seek permission, further information about the Publisher's permissions policies and our arrangements with organizations such as the Copyright Clearance Center and the Copyright Licensing Agency, can be found at our website: www.elsevier.com/permissions.

This book and the individual contributions contained in it are protected under copyright by the Publisher (other than as may be noted herein).

Notices
Knowledge and best practice in this field are constantly changing. As new research and experience broaden our understanding, changes in research methods or professional practices, may become necessary. Practitioners and researchers must always rely on their own experience and knowledge in evaluating and using any information or methods described herein. In using such information or methods they should be mindful of their own safety and the safety of others, including parties for whom they have a professional responsibility.

To the fullest extent of the law, neither the Publisher nor the authors, contributors, or editors, assume any liability for any injury and/or damage to persons or property as a matter of products liability, negligence or otherwise, or from any use or operation of any methods, products, instructions, or ideas contained in the material herein.

Library of Congress Cataloging-in-Publication Data
Application submitted

British Library Cataloguing-in-Publication Data
A catalogue record for this book is available from the British Library.

ISBN: 978-0-12-420245-0

For information on all MK publications
visit our website at www.mkp.com

Working together
to grow libraries in
developing countries

www.elsevier.com • www.bookaid.org

Dedication

This book is dedicated to Rob Veltre, Jr., my boss, coworker, and good friend of 13 years. Every interaction designer hopes for an enlightened, C-level champion of design within their organization. Rob has been that for me, living his mantra: "Build the thing right. But first, make sure you build the right thing." In an engineering-centric company, he was the one who best understood the value I brought to a project and how to make the most of it. He supported me when I needed authority, and he pushed me when I needed to stretch myself. It is in no small part due to Rob's nurturing of me and the developers I work with that I have collected the experience and knowledge necessary to write this book. It has been an honor to work for him and a pleasure to work with him.

Contents

Acknowledgments

I want to thank Brian Cavalier for introducing me to OOCSS and for his role as reviewer of this book. I may not have reached the technical understanding that enabled me to develop my workshop without him. I also appreciate the other reviewers who ensured the validity and applicability of my writing: Matt Nish-Lapidus as reviewer of the book, and Grant Carmichael and Erik Dahl as reviewers of the proposal.

Many of my Inmedius coworkers have influenced my writing, but I would especially like to recognize Will Ross, Steven Schwab, Kelly Dolan, Joe D'Alessandro, Henry Burke, Jeff Christensen, and Doug Fellner.

Finally, I owe my wife Susie, and my daughters Felicity and Genevieve, a debt for the attention this book stole from them.

Preface

As tends to happen with experience, my convictions have morphed over the course of my career. As a graduate student studying interaction design at Carnegie Mellon University (CMU), I was of the opinion that designers shouldn't need to know how to code. We should have tools that give us complete freedom to create without requiring knowledge of the technical bits that are necessary to realize our visions. Looking back at my younger self, it seems hypocritical. I had already learned the technical process of offset printing—not enough to set up and run a press, mind you, but enough to know the difference between process and spot colors, how to specify them, and how to design a brochure with only two colors to keep the cost down. I knew that I had to include an extra margin if I wanted an image to bleed off the edge of the page. As it turns out, I had to learn a lot about the production process to be an effective graphic designer. Why did I not expect to have to do the same to effectively design for the web?

I was quickly disabused of the notion once I took a job with a software development firm where I was expected to hand over HTML that developers could cut and paste into their Java server pages (JSPs). My screens may have looked fine, but the what-you-see-is-what-you-get (WYSIWYG) editor I was using generated terribly ugly code. So it was that I began down a path that resulted in the book you hold in your hands now. But it isn't just a book about code. More important than learning how to write clean Cascading Style Sheets (CSS) is learning how to integrate with your development team.

You see, when I was first hired by that small software development firm, I was set to work on a complete, ground-up redesign of their flagship product. This was to happen in parallel with the development team rearchitecting the product. The company was young, and I was inexperienced. I was advised by another designer who had been with the company since its inception to not show my work to the developers until I had polished it to perfection. I'm sure you already sense the train wreck that was coming. Sure enough, after months of brainstorming new features and iterating over pixel-perfect screen mockups, I presented my work to the developers, only to be told, "Hey, that looks great, but our architecture assumed the same functionality and a similar interface to what we have now." They were too far down their side of the tunnel to come back for me, so my fully designed and specified user interface (UI) was shelved. I learned a valuable lesson the hard way, and since then, I've worked diligently to integrate myself tightly as part of the development team. Doing so has paid great dividends, and I'd very much like to share them with you.

I've now been working for that same company over 13 years, during which time I've been able to merge my design process with that of the developers.

I use many of the same tools they use for task assignment, issue tracking, version control, and documentation. Where once upon a time I would hand over my designs to the developers for implementation, I now participate in implementation, ensuring that every detail of the design is translated correctly by contributing directly to the production code base. And that brings us full circle. If you want total control of your design, from its first inspiration to the day the finished product ships (not to mention future revisions), you have to participate in the entire development process. That means you should be able to write production-ready HTML and CSS. That's why I decided to write a book that is one part down-and-dirty code tutorial and the other part ideological process and collaboration. Both parts give practical advice, some of which you can put into action immediately, and some you can begin to plan and build toward.

One person who has the skills of a visual designer, an interaction designer, and front-end web developer is often referred to in our industry as a unicorn—a magical, mythical creature and the object of many a great hunt. If you look at natural history, you'll find many plausible origins for the legend of the unicorn. You'll also find a number of creatures that, while not matching our perfect envisioning of a unicorn, are nonetheless creatures with four legs and a single horn. I posit that there are actually quite a few designers in the workforce who meet the base-level description of a unicorn; they just don't have the opportunity or direction necessary to meet their full potential. Perhaps you are one of them? My sincere hope is that this book will be the incentive that leads you to take that next pivotal step in your career.

PART I

Working with Developers for Fun and Profit

"The way we work at Apple is that the complexity of these products really makes it critical to work collaboratively, with different areas of expertise. I think that's one of the things about my job I enjoy the most. I work with silicon designers, electronic and mechanical engineers, and I think you would struggle to determine who does what when we get together. We're located together, we share the same goal, have exactly the same preoccupation with making great products."

Sir Jonathan Ive

Jony is speaking of his collaborations as an industrial designer, but the same sentiment should apply to the way we, as interaction designers, work with developers. The tighter we can integrate with our development teams, the more effective we can be in our efforts to deliver good experiences to our users. It stands to reason that the closer we work with developers, the better our products will be. Better products hopefully result in better sales. As a result, we profit from improved collaboration. That's one way to look at it, but money is only part of the equation. A paycheck isn't enough to keep us satisfied in our employment. If you are anything like me, the relationships you have with your coworkers contribute significantly to any decisions about how long you stay at a company. Developing better relationships with developers, then, is going to increase our enjoyment of our day-to-day activities. Have your cake and eat it too; work with developers for fun *and* profit.

State of the Industry

1

In the latter half of 2011, I was putting together a conference presentation on the topic of working with developers. I was hypothesizing that the majority of designers weren't integrated well with their developers, but I was working purely off of anecdotal evidence. I figured I should get a more accurate picture of the state of the industry, so I published an online survey through Survs and advertised it to the Interaction Design Association (IxDA), the AIGA Experience mailing list, through my own blog, and a few other channels. While over 300 people viewed the survey, only 82 respondents completed it. I realize that's not a big data set, and I don't claim to be a statistician, but I do believe that the results I'm presenting here are representative of the design community. For the most part, the results confirmed my suspicions, but I also found some really interesting outcomes I wasn't expecting. At the very least, they convinced me that there's a need for the information that I'm disseminating at conferences and now in book form. The full data set is available on GitHub at *https://github.com/jackmoffett/Bridging-UX-and-Web-Development/*. If you do anything further with the results or have additional thoughts on the conclusions I'm sharing here, I encourage you to drop me a line and share your thoughts.

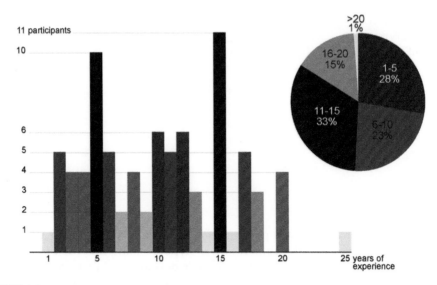

FIGURE 1.1

Years of experience

The survey respondents were evenly distributed in their years of experience in the field, almost equally split between those with 10 or less years and those with more than 10 years. I had expected a lower percentage in the over 10 group, but I was pleased to see that my results evenly spanned the experience continuum. Further checking showed that there weren't any significant trends based on experience, so there's no need to show you any of the results broken down in that fashion. You can assume that for the rest of the survey questions, the answers were evenly distributed, experience-wise.

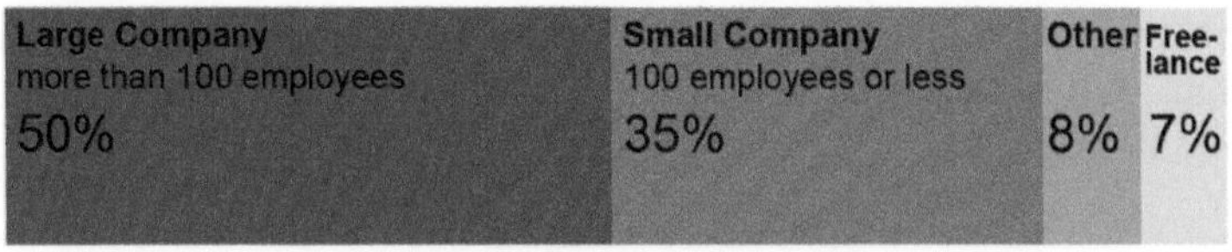

Large Company more than 100 employees	Small Company 100 employees or less	Other	Free-lance
50%	35%	8%	7%

FIGURE 1.2

Company size

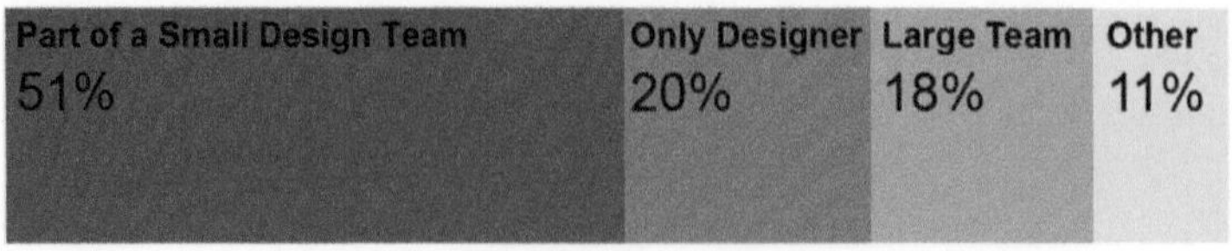

Part of a Small Design Team	Only Designer	Large Team	Other
51%	20%	18%	11%

FIGURE 1.3

Design team size

To provide context, participants were asked about their current work situations. Exactly half of the respondents worked in a company larger than 100 employees, while only 7% were freelancers. At the same time, about half of the respondents were part of a small design team. In retrospect, I probably should have specified ranges for team size the way I did company size, but we'll have to work with the resultant ambiguity.

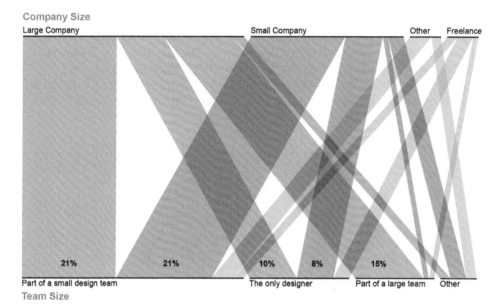

FIGURE 1.4

Company size versus team size

When viewed as a parallel set, you can see from the figures that the most common case is to be working as part of a small design team, either within a large company or small company. And while it's more common to be the only designer than to work in a large design group, that's only because half of the freelancers are included in the count. There are a similar number of respondents (within three percentage points) working in a large design group within a large company as there are working as the only designer within a company, large or small. This is relevant information, as it shows that the majority of the respondents are in a work environment that my survey was specifically designed to address—that is, an organization in which designers have the opportunity to collaborate with developers on a daily basis. Consultants who only work with any given project team for a short time will find it harder to integrate at the level I'm promoting. Similarly, design firms that don't staff their own developers are less likely to integrate at all. That doesn't mean that it isn't worth attempting, only that it'll require more attention and flexibility.

Software Development Firm	Other	UX/Design
44%	39%	17%

FIGURE 1.5

How would you classify your company?

I found it particularly interesting that 39% of respondents worked for companies that weren't software development or design firms. The prevalence of designers embedded within product and service companies is a good indicator of the acceptance of design as a necessary contributor. For the purposes of this survey, it gives us an interesting point of comparison for some of the following questions.

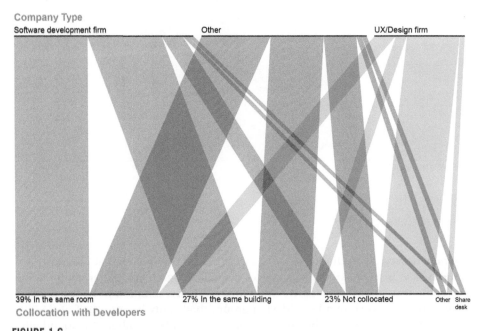

Company Type

Software development firm · Other · UX/Design firm

39% In the same room · 27% In the same building · 23% Not collocated · Other Share desk

Collocation with Developers

FIGURE 1.6

Company type versus collocation with developers

As you can clearly see in the parallel set in Figure 1.6, the majority of respondents who work for a design firm aren't collocated with developers (the thickest teal band). Of course, the vast majority of those working at a software development firm are collocated and are evenly divided between being in the same room or elsewhere within the same building. When it comes to designers embedded in a product/service company, most share a room with the developers. Two respondents actually share a desk with a developer. That seems a bit extreme—you both have my sympathy.

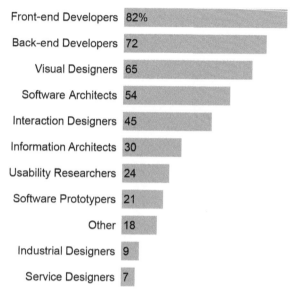

Front-end Developers	82%
Back-end Developers	72
Visual Designers	65
Software Architects	54
Interaction Designers	45
Information Architects	30
Usability Researchers	24
Software Prototypers	21
Other	18
Industrial Designers	9
Service Designers	7

FIGURE 1.7

Who do you work with on a regular basis?

Figure 1.7 shows what other job roles respondents work with on a regular basis: 82% work with front-end developers, and 72% work with back-end developers. Those are the two most prevalent collaborations, with visual designers coming in third.

To summarize what we've learned so far, we can generalize that most interaction designers and user experience (UX) professionals are working for companies in which they're collocated with developers and collaborate with them more than anyone else. That says to me that we should be spending a lot more time in design education and professional development teaching designers how to work with developers. When you look at typical design schools, however, you'll find very little cross-discipline collaboration. And looking at most design conference programs, there isn't much in the way of designer–developer relations, although it's more often a topic for discussion in the Agile community.

With that understanding, let's examine what exactly these designers are doing, as shown in Figure 1.8.

Most of the respondents (86%) claimed to be competent interaction designers. That's not at all surprising, given that the survey was advertised to them. UI prototyping comes in at 55%, but the number drops to 18% for actual

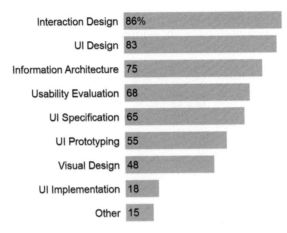

FIGURE 1.8

Skill competency

implementation. Now, just because we're proficient at something doesn't mean we're using that skill in our current position. I'd claim to be a competent illustrator and photographer if they were listed, but I don't use those skills very often in my job. Figure 1.9 details what activities respondents regularly participate in.

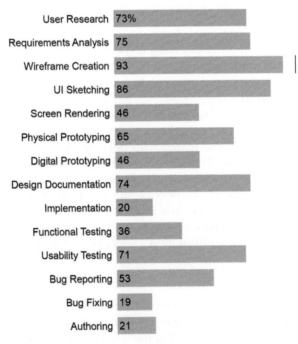

FIGURE 1.9

Activity participation

Wireframe creation and UI sketching are the top two activities. This is exactly what I was expecting. Design documentation, requirements analysis, user research, and usability testing all come in the lower seventieth percentile. Physical prototyping, at 65%, surprised me by beating out digital prototyping and screen rendering, both of which were below 50%. Perhaps that speaks to the recent popularity of paper prototyping for mobile devices. Now we get down to the activities I'm most interested in. Only half of the respondents are reporting bugs. That's a missed opportunity I'll discuss later. Very much related to bug reporting is participation in functional testing—that is, testing the product to make sure everything works as intended. Only 20% are participating in implementation, but to be honest, that's a little higher than I was afraid it might be. At 19%, it appears that most of the designers who are implementing their UIs are also fixing their bugs, so that's good.

All-in-all, the survey results confirmed my suspicions. Most designers don't implement the UIs they design, but they do work with the developers on a regular basis, hopefully ensuring that the integrity of their design is translated into the functioning product. On the other hand, there's a sizable number of designers who are participating in implementation. Here's where things get really interesting.

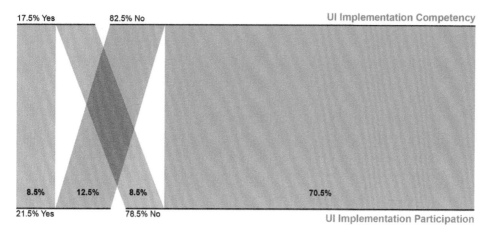

FIGURE 1.10

Implementation competency versus participation

Figure 1.10 is a simple parallel set that tells us two things. First, half of the designers who consider themselves competent in the skills necessary to implement a UI don't regularly participate in implementation as part of their jobs. We can postulate reasons. They may work in a team that has specialized front-end developers capable of understanding the nuances of visual design (typography, color, etc.) who are technically more capable than the designers in question. Given the rarity of us unicorns, however, I'd be surprised if that's a significant reason. More likely, their developers don't have any expectation that the designers would contribute production code, and the designers haven't made an effort to do so. They may feel uncomfortable trying to insert themselves into the unfamiliar development process. In some cases, there may even be hostilities between the two groups. This group of designers I feel uniquely qualified to help. If you're one, well, hello there! This book is written especially for you.

Second, Figure 1.10 shows us that over half of the designers regularly participating in implementation don't consider themselves to be competent. I can imagine quite a lot of reasons for that feeling as well, from lack of familiarity with tools and process, to relationships, to doubts about the quality of the code they produce. It just so happens that I can help the designers who find themselves in that boat too. Welcome aboard! This book was written especially for you. *Shhhh—I just told those other folks the same thing.*

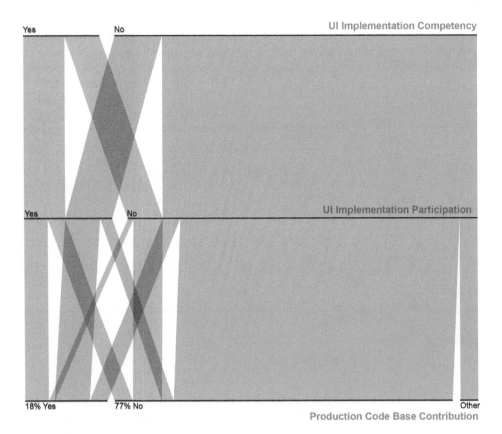

FIGURE 1.11

Implementation competency versus participation versus production code

There's more to this picture, though. Just because you participate in implementation doesn't mean you contribute directly to the production code base. For a long time, I was generating HTML, as full screens or partial snippets, and handing it off to the developers. There's nothing wrong with that, per se, but it's not optimal, and we'll come back to that in later chapters. It's better when the designer is putting her own code into the application, testing it, tweaking it, and committing it to the repository.

Expanding out the parallel set we started with in Figure 1.10, we can trace the answers to those first two questions and see how the same respondents then answered the question as to whether or not they work directly in the production code base. I'll highlight the two groups for you to make it easier to see what's going on.

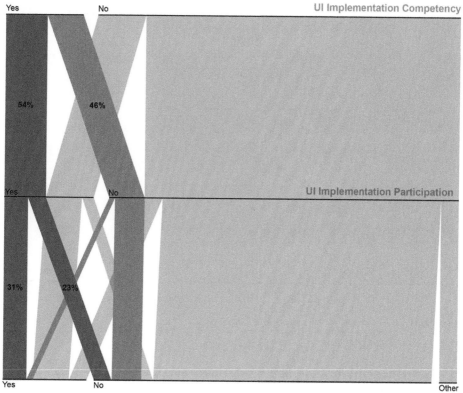

FIGURE 1.12

Designers who are competent implementers

Those in red consider themselves competent implementers. Just under half of them don't participate in implementation. Of those who do, almost half don't contribute directly to the production code base. Note that one respondent claims to contribute directly to the production code base without participating in implementation. That's not possible, so I'll consider it an error, one way or the other. So, where the rubber meets the road, only 31% of the capable implementers are reaching their full potential.

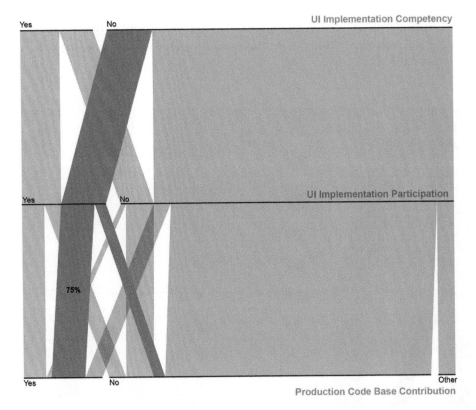

FIGURE 1.13

Designers who aren't competent implementers

Then we have our blue designers, the ones who—I don't want to call them incompetent—don't feel qualified to implement their designs. I've highlighted just the ones who participate in implementation anyway—10% of our total respondents. The majority of those (75%) are contributing directly to the production code base.

So there you have it. This is the current state of the web design profession. *There are more unqualified designers contributing production code than there are qualified designers, while less than half of those who are qualified to contribute actually do so!*

This situation must be remedied, and it all starts with relationships.

Looking for Group

2

It's not surprising that the workplace is such rich fodder for situation comedies. You don't usually have a choice as to whom you end up having to work with, and you must interact with those people nine to five, five days a week (or thereabout). The last question of the survey asked participants about the relationships they have with their developers. It's good to know that the majority of respondents enjoy mutual respect. Around half indicated friendships.

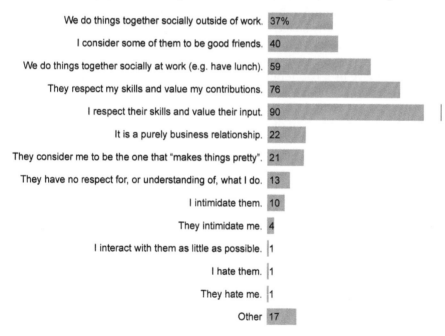

FIGURE 2.1

What kind of relationship do you have with the developers you work with?

Bridging UX and Web Development
© 2014 Elsevier Inc. All rights reserved.

Of course, there are also those that don't get along so well. There is a fair amount of misunderstanding on the developers' parts as to the role of a designer, and there is some intimidation on both sides. One respondent expressed confusion, commenting, "Sometimes I feel as though they truly appreciate a human-centered approach to software/web development, and at other times, I feel as though they think that the design process is a lot of unnecessary fluff." A few people stated that it varies greatly from one developer to another. Now, I'm not a psychologist, and I'm not going to pretend to have a deep reservoir of knowledge about interpersonal relationships. There are plenty of books out there about that. What I *can* offer is some wisdom I've accumulated over 15 years working closely with software engineers. If you want to improve your professional relationship with your development team, I think I can share some worthwhile advice. If you want to date one of them, well, I can't promise this book will help you there, but it won't hurt.

DO'S AND DON'TS OF DESIGNER–DEVELOPER RELATIONSHIPS

1. **Don't critique engineering prototypes on aesthetics or usability.**

    We designers tend to be rather critical people. It's one of the traits that make us particularly suited to what we do. We sweat the details because we care. Sometimes, we find it hard to suppress our natural tendency to critique everything we see based on the high standards to which we hold ourselves. That can give us a bad reputation as being arrogant and condescending. Understand that the purpose of an engineering prototype is to prove a technical approach and expose potential issues before implementation starts. It's designed to prove or disprove developers' theories about such aspects as performance, security, or difficulty. It's certainly not meant to be attractive, and it only has to be usable by the developers themselves. The whole point is to do as little work as possible as quickly as possible to learn as much as necessary. Providing design-oriented feedback on such a prototype will only show the developers that you don't understand technology and perpetuate the stereotype of designers as pretentious, overbearing fops.

2. **Don't expect developers to have the same design sensibilities you have.**

    Most developers have had no visual training. They don't likely understand the intricacies of typography, and the extent of their knowledge of color theory may be that yellow on blue provides the most contrast. This is likely obvious, and they'd probably readily admit it, telling you that they did terribly in art class and can't draw worth a darn. So, why would you hold that against them? I certainly wouldn't want the developers I work with to snicker at my paltry mathematical skills or disregard me due to my misunderstanding a regex. I'm happy to laugh about it with them as long as they don't disrespect me because of it. Show your developers the respect they deserve for what they're good at.

3. Don't force your process on the developers.

    Just as we have a process we prefer to follow, along with methods and tools that support it, so too the developers have been trained in their own process. Trying to make them change the way they do things outright is likely going to be met with hostility. After all, what would your response be if your development team told you that they believe sketching is a waste of time, and they want you to start working directly in code? You'd probably tell them they could go stick their code in their .ear. But we need to work together. In the next chapter, I'll be presenting a collaboration life cycle that marries a typical interaction design process with a standard software development process. Don't try to force it on them all at once. Rather, find ways to start inserting yourself. As they begin to see improvements, you'll build trust, eventually reaching a point at which you can begin suggesting changes that they'll consider. Work toward long-term goals instead of pushing for immediate favor.

4. Don't expect developers to make last-minute changes just because you haven't been involved until late in the process.

    Yes, it's an unfortunate situation, and the product is going to suffer, but you won't be doing anyone any favors by trying to bully the developers into reimplementing things when they're already under the gun to complete implementation on time. Instead of self-righteously declaring the product crap and stubbornly insisting that x and y have to be redone, analyze the current state, identifying low-hanging fruit. Prioritize it based on what will benefit the users the most. Then, meet with the lead developer, assuring him that you're there to help as best you can. Present the options and discuss what might be possible given the remaining man-hours. Some of it may even be admissible as bugs that can be worked on during functional testing. Be satisfied in the knowledge that you have provided a service and positively impacted the product—one that the developers are likely to start seeking out sooner—even if the end result isn't something you're otherwise proud of. Banking developer goodwill will eventually pay back great dividends.

5. Position your involvement as something that makes your developers' jobs easier.

    Developers have a lot to worry about. Like anyone, there are some things they prefer to think about more than others. We're the same way. It works out quite well, because, generally speaking, the things we want to spend our time thinking about are the very things they'd rather not have to, and vice versa. When it comes to architecting and building software, most developers prefer to know exactly what they have to implement. They don't want to have to make a bunch of decisions about how a function should manifest in the UI. They'd prefer to dig into the technical challenges facing them, which is why they typically implement the first widget that comes to mind, if it isn't already specified. Nor do they want to spend time trying to interpret a customer's obtuse requirements. The developers I work with are elated to have me work with the customer (or our own product managers) to flesh out the requirements, nail down the details, and turn them into a specification that can be accurately estimated. If I'm ensuring that we're building the right thing, they can spend their brain cells on building the thing right.

6. Be inclusive.

   As I said before, the developers appreciate my involvement, but it's not my place to dictate the entirety of the product. I don't have all the answers, and without the developers' input, I'm likely to turn out an application that's too expensive to build, too performance intensive, or just wrong because I misunderstood something. I ask the developers I work with for feedback on my designs much as I would another designer, and I encourage their questions. When a developer offers an idea for the UI, I walk through it with them. It's the perfect opportunity to educate them (see #8). If there are problems with the idea, I explain them. Sometimes, it's a better idea than I had, and I graciously accept it, telling them that it's a great idea, and "I don't know why I didn't think of that myself." It isn't the designer's job to make decisions so much as to offer options. Rely on the collective wisdom of the team to choose the best ones.

7. Dare to compromise.

   All too often, the best design is the hardest to implement. Presenting the most useful information may result in the least-efficient database calls. The best user experience may be the least secure. The most effective interaction may take the most time and effort to build. Given the constraints of budget and schedule, we can't always have the best of all worlds. Learn to pick your battles. What's so important it's worth fighting for? What's worth giving up to keep the project on track? What tradeoffs are worth making to maintain the entire team's sanity while still delivering a quality product? If you show that you're willing to compromise, the developers you work with will be much more likely to do the same.

8. Find opportunities to educate.

   I've always considered design evangelism to be an important part of my job—so much so, I wrote it into my job description. Teaching my customers and coworkers about design raises the perceived value of my involvement. Teaching the developers I work with about design allows them to appreciate my contribution. I accomplish this informally through discussions and collaborative decision making, as well as more formally through brown-bag lunch presentations. I often include the reasoning behind decisions in my design documentation, and I encourage questions. When a developer challenges your design, your first instinct may be to act defensive. I've certainly shown some indignation toward developers sticking their noses into my business, but that's a selfish attitude that isn't going to help anyone. Give their criticism due consideration. If it's valid, thank them, and congratulate them on catching your gaff. If you believe your design to be valid, explain to them exactly why.

9. Be social.

    This may seem obvious, but it's worth stating anyway. True relationships, even professional ones, depend on people getting to know each other. For those of you lucky enough to work in a group of designers (69%), it's probably easy to spend your time socializing with your like-minded cohorts while keeping interactions with your developers on purely business terms. As a designer in the opposite situation, I'm here to report that, believe it or not, software engineers are people too. They do have lives outside the office, and once you move the subject away from JAXP or regression tests, they can carry on a normal conversation. I've developed lasting friendships with some of the developers I've had the pleasure to work with that I've carried on even after they left the company. When they have professional development lunches, I participate, and I've presented at some. I even sat in on one or two of their Java certification study sessions. I've been instrumental in maintaining a tradition of going out to eat together for lunch every Friday. And I'm not embarrassed to admit that I play World of Warcraft with a couple of them. Yes, I even socialize with them outside of work. This should be the natural, human thing to do, but if you need more practical convincing, think of this: it's much harder to ignore somebody's feelings when you know you'll be sitting across from them at lunch. Your developers will treat you better if you're truly a part of the team, rather than one more outsider telling them what to do. Jenna Bilotta expresses this well in her article *"How Designers and Engineers Can Play Nice (and Still Run with Scissors)"*:

> Have a beer with your engineer. You can accelerate trust and communication if someone feels you care about them as a person—and not just a set of skills that you rely on to realize a design vision.

    Of course, relationships are a two-way street. There's only so much you can do to encourage the developers you work with to reciprocate. For advice on working with a designer as an engineer, I recommend checking out Uday Gajendar's presentations on the subject (*http://youtu.be/aS5vIXbRvOU*).

DEVELOPER PERSONAS

General advice is all well and good, but let's get a little more specific. In fact, let's apply a little design methodology to this problem. I've worked with a lot of developers, and I've been able to classify some of their common traits. Read through these personas and see if you can find the developers you work with.

The old dogs

One trend I found in the survey results supports my own personal experience working with developers. The older the developer, the more likely he will be difficult to work with. I realize that's a very generalized statement, and it depends on the individual, but take the following comment one designer left on the survey:

I find there to be a difference between some of the older developers and younger developers. The older ones are a little confused by my role as an interaction designer. The younger ones really seem to value my input and user-centered design processes. They're excited about the changes and like to contribute new ideas. The older developers who seem to have a different school of thought start shaking their head as soon as I stop by their desk with a fresh stack of sketches.

This is likely a case of people being set in their ways. They have been practicing their profession without an interaction designer for years, so why do they need one now? Another survey participant said:

It seems to be a matter of how long people have been here. The folks who have been here longer seem to resent my addition to the team and cause the most problems. The newer people don't seem to have a problem with my work.

Of course, it's much easier for new hires to accept an interaction designer as part of an established process. That's their baseline as they become indoctrinated to the company's culture. Contrast that with a UX professional hired into a company that doesn't already have a design-oriented culture. There's a huge difference:

Its the old-school developers who are the hardest to work with. It seems like from their viewpoint, there's no reason why they shouldn't be doing the design work.

So, how can you turn this situation into a mutually beneficial working relationship? I don't have any magic dust—it's likely going to be difficult—but rest assured that with patience and perseverance, it's possible to gain the respect of the senior developers and pull them over to the light side. I've done it. Meet John Stern.

John Stern
Senior Software Architect

- Holds a Ph.D. in computer science.

- Knows he's smarter than you.

- Philosophy behind architecture of the system trumps all.

- Set in his ways, like an old dog.

- Highly risk-averse, so he doesn't like trying anything new.

- Doesn't really care about design, because he doesn't care about the UI or the user.

- The first time you ask him if you can do something, he immediately says "No." Ten minutes later, he comes back and explains how you can do it and why it'll work.

- Ultimately, he is more interested in publishing a paper about the software architecture than delivering the product.

John may be the hardest developer for you to learn to work with. He's going to cause you to mutter under your breath on a daily basis. Here's my advice for turning what seems to be an impossible situation to your advantage:

- Show him some respect. He has earned it, and while he may be misguided, he's no idiot. Don't try to play top dog, because he'll fight you for it. I'm not saying you should be submissive, but treat him as an equal. Don't play the superior, I-know-something-you-don't-know type of designer who we're so good at.

- Let him know your credentials. He has a lot of respect for higher education, so he may give you a few bonus points and the benefit of the doubt if he knows you have a degree.

- Try to couch your design decisions as solutions to *his* problems. Convincing him that you're going to make his life easier should be your number-one goal in this relationship.

- Learn to read UML diagrams. Speaking his language will not only improve communications and earn you some rep, but it'll give you a better understanding of how your designs fit into the overall picture.

- When trying to introduce something new, preempt his rejections by providing supporting evidence: examples of use, code samples, and any requirements, such as versions, incompatibilities, and the like. He'll take your suggestions more seriously if you show that you've done some research into their feasibility.

- Be patient. Try not to be confrontational. He may never fully appreciate your contribution, but he may come to respect you for your process, rigor, and attention to detail. Those are things he can relate to.

The designer wannabe

A lot of developers care nothing for UI work, while others enjoy working on the part of the software that people can actually see. Occasionally you get a developer who is design-curious. Maybe he took an HCI course in school, saw a TED talk that resonated with him, or has worked with designers in the past. Many designers would be annoyed with, or threatened by, a developer who wants to do our job, but I recommend embracing him. Allow me to introduce you to Reece.

Reece Groene
Software Engineer II

- Loves to do UI work. Where many of his colleagues prefer the back-end stuff, Reece prefers spending his time on the part of the software that people will actually see.

- Always happy to take a first crack at the UI. He won't wait for you to deliver sketches.

- Excited when the designer comes up with improvements.

- Will work his butt off to implement a difficult UI because he believes in it.

While you may initially feel like Reece is invading your turf, this guy can be your best friend. He understands enough about the UI to recognize that your designs are better than what he comes up with, and he's dedicated to getting it working correctly. Here's my advice for developing a good working relationship with him and using these traits to your advantage:

- Don't rain on his parade. Don't immediately shoot his ideas down every time he does something on his own. Sit down and do a constructive critique. Explain why his decisions aren't good ones, and pick out anything that's worth keeping, or at least considering, for the final design.

- You may even take him under your wing—start teaching him how you go about designing. There are many good designers who started as coders and few designers who have coding as a strength. You might end up training a new design team member with a very helpful skill set.

- When you're looking for feedback on your UI designs, run them by Reece. This will help build mutual respect, showing him that you do care about his opinion and recognize his interest and expertise in the UI. He may even give you some good ideas.

- Whenever you're unsure about the feasibility of one of your own designs or the capabilities of a particular technology, consult with Reece first. He'll have a good sense of what your concerns are and what you're trying to accomplish and for what reasons. He'll understand the technical problem from your perspective and may be able to offer alternatives that wouldn't occur to another developer (like John).

In time, Reece may come to see you as a mentor. He'll at least respect you as an equal. And with his drive to make the UI the best it can be, he'll be a great asset for you. One of the survey respondents had this to say about the developers he or she works with:

Yes, they actively provide feedback about the visual design, as well as the information architecture. They're much more informed than people think. They also care about these details much more than they're credited for.

The young hipster

The antithesis of the old dog, some developers are really excited about the potential of new technology and willing to try just about anything. They may well be the easiest to get along with, so you won't likely need my advice. Let's include Will here anyway, for the sake of completeness.

Will Jameson
Software Engineer III

- Has a master's degree.

- Technology is frickin' cool!

- Not afraid to try new things, especially early in the development cycle.

- Always checking out the latest toolkit, application, or device, and wants to use them.

- Gets stuff done.

- Takes pride in his work, but doesn't over think things.

- Perfectly willing to trash his code and start over, because he knows he can do it better, faster.

- Tends to underestimate how much work something will actually be.

- Design is cool too, because it makes the things he does even cooler.

With such a positive attitude, it'd be hard to screw up this relationship. Here's how to make the most of it:

- Go to Will first with any questions you have about the feasibility of an idea. He won't start with "no."

- When you present a design that may be difficult to implement, all you have to do is show him an example of it done elsewhere. He'll figure it out from there.

- Learning Will's limits will also be important. You may have to temper his enthusiasm at times.

- He'll be more than happy to show you how to use any of the tools the development team employs, and he'll get you set up so you can check the latest build whenever you want.

- Perhaps best of all, Will is going to treat you as an equal from the start. You don't have to prove yourself to him. If you're competent, he'll accept you as a like mind.

The super-efficient project manager

Of all the developers, this is the one that you definitely want to be on good terms with. She can make your job a true joy, or she can make you seriously think about moving on. Fortunately, she is fairly easy to get along with, once you understand what makes her tick. Enter Shelley, stage right.

Shelley Stevens
Project Lead

- Married to the burn-down chart. As long as the lines are converging, she's peachy keen.

- The schedule is king, so try not to push it.

- Process is queen, so try to follow it. Make good suggestions for improving it, and she'll be thrilled.

- Stickler for details.

- Expects perfection in the code, as well as in your specifications.

- Follows specifications to the letter.

- Appreciates working with a good interaction designer, because she doesn't have to make decisions about what should be built. She can focus on how to build it.

- Works to her estimates. If she perceives difficulty in the design, she'll ask for a compromise.

All of these traits are good traits, even if she seems a little overbearing at times. All of these traits can serve the concerns of design and usability well if you keep the following in mind:

- More than any, Shelley is the developer you want to have involved in design activity. The sooner she knows what you have in mind, the more likely your plans will fit into the schedule. She'll also ask the right questions that will help you turn out a complete, feasible specification.

- She has a closer connection to the customer than the other developers, so she understands the importance of satisfying them.

- Give her an understanding of the users, and she'll become sympathetic to usability issues as well.

- While her mantra may be "difficulty in implementation compromises efficiency," she'll reluctantly give in to requests for additional work if you can make a good case for it.

- Compromise. If you're willing to do this, you can pick your battles. She'll give a little if you're reasonable and there's some slack in the schedule.

- Of course, the rest of the team has to do what she says, so even if she's the only one you regularly eat lunch with, you've got it made. *(Pssst. That comment was made tongue-in-cheek. You really want to play well with all team members.)*

The spastic genius

This is the guy who will keep you humble. Cherish him.

**Harry D'Angelo
Technical Lead**

- Brilliant engineer.

- Fast talker—he's hard to follow.

- Very friendly, but humble to a fault.

- He'll talk your ear off, apologize for doing so, and change topics in the same breath.

- Is usually thinking about five steps ahead of you.

- Will remember the requirements better than you do.

- Will remember your design specs better than you do and will point out inconsistencies.

- Will ask you all of the questions about your design that you should have already answered.

- Thinks through a problem ahead of time, so when he comes to you with a question, he dives right into the details without giving you any context.

I know, he sounds kind of annoying. He's occasionally going to embarrass you. But you know what? He's going to make you a better designer. You're going to end up making fewer mistakes, being more consistent, and better organized, because you know that he'll catch you if you aren't. And he's not malicious—it's just the way he is wired. This is how you work with Harry:

- Always keep your requirements and specification documents within reach. When Harry shows up, pull them out. You're going to need them to make sure you're both talking about the same screen, feature, or even application.

- If you don't know what he's talking about immediately, don't let him ramble. Tell him to stop, take a breath, slow down, and give you some context.

- Use your screen mockups to focus the discussion.

- Use a whiteboard or sketch on paper during discussions with him to keep things visual and ensure you're understanding him.

- Try to include him in all of your UI design reviews. Your product will be better for it.

- Be gracious. Thank him for his contributions. Let him know that you're someone who will always listen to him. After all, if he's going to tell someone about problems with the UI design, it may as well be you.

So, there you have it. Getting along with developers isn't rocket science, or computer science, but it's important if you want to have more control over the final form of the application, and quite frankly, you're going to enjoy your job a whole lot more if you're friends with the people you work with. Now that we've dealt with relationships, let's take a look at an aspect of working with developers that's a lot less nebulous: process. I like to call it the "collaboration life cycle."

Collaboration Life Cycle

3

Process. Regardless of what type of designer you are—graphic, information, interaction, service, industrial, game—you follow a common process. It typically begins with research and observation as you learn about the people who will use the product of your efforts and the context of its use. Then there's synthesizing of the information you've collected, coupled with ideation and iterative prototyping, as you plan what is to be built, physically, digitally, or figuratively. Ideally, this also involves some form of testing with users to verify your rationale. As I illustrated in Chapter 1, this is where many of us stop, passing our specifications on to the developers who will implement the work. There are also varying degrees of participation in following phases of testing, bug fixing, and further documentation. Of course, there are sundry variations, Agile and Lean UX being the most notable, but the same activities are involved (or should be).

Let me stop here for a moment to address the Agile elephant, because if I don't, I know it'll stomp ominously about the periphery of the room and distract us from important matters. I don't follow an Agile process most of the time, although I've worked on projects that did. I don't have problems with the Agile philosophy, as I understand it, and I have a lot of respect for my peers in the industry who have been successful at adapting their design practices to it. If you find yourself working in an Agile environment, I recommend that you check out one of their books on the matter. I'm not an expert on Agile methods, and this book will not specifically address them. That said, I consider the collaboration life cycle I describe here to be somewhat process agnostic. I believe that designers should be involved in every phase of development, and whether your organization follows a waterfall model, Agile, or something in between as mine does, you should be thinking about how you can incorporate the following activities into your process. To read more of my thoughts on Lean UX, I invite you to visit my blog, DesignAday, where I've addressed the topic in some depth: *http://designaday.tumblr.com/tagged/lean-ux.*

REQUIREMENTS ANALYSIS

During the first phase of a project, designers are learning as much as they can about the domain. We're doing whatever kinds of user research that time, the budget, and the client allow. We may be creating personas, writing scenarios, or any number of other information-gathering and synthesizing tasks. There's a lot to do, and it's easy for us to forget about the developers during this time. After all, this is where UX professionals shine. We realize the importance of ensuring that we're building the right thing. But we shouldn't ignore the developers, busy though we may be. They're collecting their own information, and we should be aware of their findings, as their decisions can greatly affect what can and can't be done.

Requirements can come from many places. If you're a subcontractor to a primary government contractor, you're probably familiar with the functional requirements document (FRD) that details all of the functions of the desired software. If you work in a software development firm that markets its own products, you may have received a marketing requirements document (MRD). If you work for a design firm, you may have encountered an enlightened client that realized that they didn't know exactly what they needed, and they relied on you to help them define their requirements. Regardless of where your requirements come from, it's imperative that you and your developers arrive at a shared understanding of the requirements.

Technical challenges

Let's say, for example, that your client has a high-level FRD outlining the basic functionality they want in a custom web application. Everyone on the project team should be familiarizing themselves with the requirements. You'll be reading them with an eye out for use cases, usability challenges, and utility, given your current understanding of their domain. Meanwhile, the developers are analyzing the requirements based on their own concerns. They'll be identifying technical challenges—features that will be more difficult or time consuming to implement. I'm reminded of the scene in the movie *Apollo 13* where the NASA engineers had to figure out a way to join the cube-shaped lithium hydroxide canisters from the command module to the lunar module's cylindrical canister-sockets using only materials found onboard: "We've got to find a way to make this... fit into the hole for this... using nothing but that." It was the proverbial square peg in a round hole.

FIGURE 3.1

The "mailbox" solution to Apollo 13's CO_2 scrubbing problem.

Photo courtesy of NASA.gov.

Technical challenges, and the approaches that the engineers decide to take, can drastically affect the amount of flexibility we have in designing the UI. We need to be aware of these challenges before we run headlong into them for two reasons. First, we don't want to waste a lot of time working on a design that has already been technically invalidated. Second, we don't want to contribute to the developers' headaches. This requires regular communication with them. Attend status meetings, keep tabs on wiki posts, and listen in on water-cooler conversations. You have a real opportunity here to ingratiate yourself with the team. Be part of the solution, rather than an aggravation of the problem. If they already know that a certain screen is going to cause performance problems, rather than blindly designing the screen in a way that compounds the issue, you can choose to learn about the problem and try to mitigate it. You might even be able to think of a different way of presenting the information that avoids the problem altogether.

When faced with a technical hurdle, developers will often create a proof-of-concept to test an approach or try out a toolkit. As I mentioned in Chapter 2, you should understand these for what they are—don't judge them as you would a design prototype. You may even be able to help with them, depending on what is being tested. For example, providing a basic UI or content display for a performance proof-of-concept could be useful. My team has had to meet strict, one-second performance requirements for delivering a screen full of data, and while retrieving the information from the database is the most important part of that, the rendering of the page in the browser plays a significant role as well. I could stick to my sketches and leave the developers to "their problem," but if I can help them shave off time by reducing the amount of DOM manipulation being done, I'll be considered an ally.

Technology stack

Another developer activity during this phase is the identification of the technology stack that will be employed on the project. This is also a matter of importance to designers. Technologies come with limitations—limitations that we have to endure as we design around them. More importantly, they're limitations that our users will have to live with. Designers need to be involved in these decisions. If your development team is considering GWT as the framework for building the front end, you had best be doing some research into its capabilities and limitations and making your opinion on the matter heard. How do you feel about the UI widgets included in GWT's library? Will they be easy to customize? Would Bootstrap and jQuery be a better approach? You'll have to learn what problems the developers think GWT will solve for them if you want to convince them of a different approach. If you choose not to participate in such decisions, you have no right blaming the developers for the resulting limitations later.

Task estimates

Have you ever been assigned to a project after the schedule is set? Maybe somebody unqualified decided how much time would be given to UI design, or perhaps they didn't account for it at all. It isn't a pleasant situation to be in. While I'm occasionally still asked to provide the design of a small change to an application at the last minute, I'm always asked to provide estimates for projects of any significance before a contract is signed. UX designers, especially those with an artistic background, are often uncomfortable doing this, but we don't help ourselves by claiming that we can't confine design to a schedule or that the creative process is too fuzzy to quantify. If we're to be taken seriously, we must do our best to support project management and help our teams deliver on time and on budget.

It's incumbent on designers to practice estimation and improve accuracy. To do this, you must be very conscious of how long it takes you to complete small, bounded tasks. Larger tasks, which may seem impossible to estimate, can be broken down into smaller tasks that can be managed. You should get in the habit of doing this, rather than throwing out random numbers from your gut that you don't know you can hit. It also requires that you track the amount of time you spend on each estimated task and compare the time you spent against your estimate. This is something that developers are experienced at doing, but designers haven't historically been required to do—certainly not in as strict a fashion.

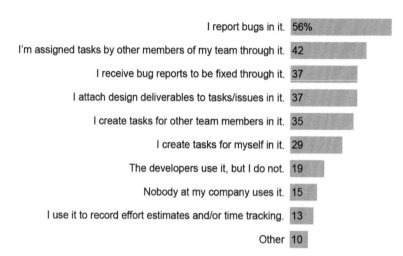

FIGURE 3.2

Task management and issue-tracking use

There are tools that developers and project managers use to track actual hours against estimated hours. I recommend that designers use the same tools. As you can see in Figure 3.2, only 13% of the survey respondents are currently doing so. Project-tracking and management software allows a team to create tasks, give each an estimate, and assign the tasks to people. My company uses Atlassian's product, JIRA, in which I enter all of my design and implementation tasks.

I provide estimates for my tasks, and as I work, I log the time I spend against each task. When I close a task upon completion, I can see whether I came in over or under my estimate. Once you've done this over the course of several projects, you'll be able to refine your estimates. Your estimates will be more accurate, and you'll be able to estimate your tasks more quickly. You'll develop better instincts for what will make certain tasks take longer than others, and you'll learn what questions you need to answer to make accurate estimates. Improving your ability to estimate will make you a better team member and increase your value to your company.

A project manager can use the reporting capabilities of the tool to track the overall progress of the team. There are different methods of doing this, of course. One common example is an hour burndown chart, which graphs out the number of estimated hours for the entire team against the number of hours logged, while also representing the number of hours the team must work each day to meet their deadline, the number of hours the team is actually working, and projecting an actual completion date. Depending on the project, the

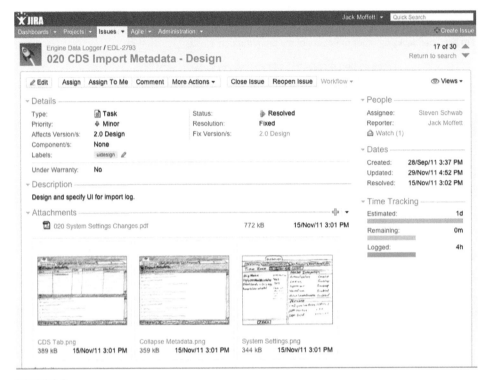

FIGURE 3.3

This is an example of a design task in Atlassian's JIRA, a project-tracking tool.

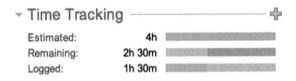

FIGURE 3.4

This graph shows my estimated hours for the task, comparing it with the time I have logged against the task and the remaining time I have to make my estimate.

manager may or may not include the designer in these calculations. If I'm not on the critical path during implementation, there's less value in my inclusion. If I'm expected to be the long pole in the tent, however, my inclusion is very valuable indeed.

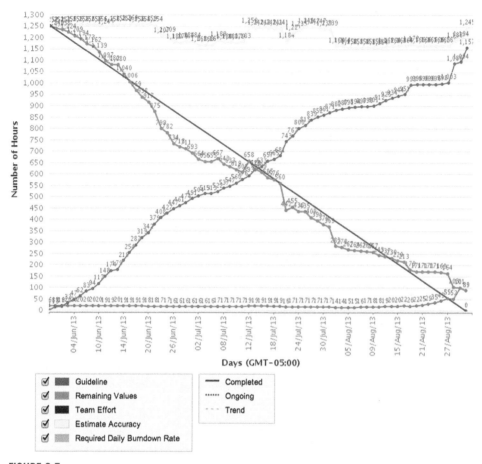

FIGURE 3.5

Hour burndown chart. The red, diagonal line represents the optimal progress against the tasks to hit the deadline exactly. The green line shows how many estimated hours are left. It should stick close to the red line; if it drops below, so much the better. The blue line indicates the cumulative amount of time the team has spent working on the project and should be the opposite of the red and green lines. The orange line at the bottom shows the number of hours the team must spend each day to make the delivery. We want that to stay low. The yellow line at the top tracks the accuracy of the team's estimates, so we'd prefer that one to stay high.

So, designers can assist the team by entering their own estimates, but let's not stop there. We can have a bigger impact by improving the accuracy of everyone's estimates. Now you may be asking, "How am I supposed to know anything about how long it's going to take developers to complete their work?" I'm not suggesting you estimate the developers' work, but designers are in a position to increase the accuracy of the developers' estimates. You see, developers are estimating how long it'll take them to implement parts of an application. For their estimates to be at all accurate, they need to have some idea of what they'll be implementing. This is another opportunity for designers to be extremely helpful to their developers. One of the survey respondents provided the following frustration in his or her comments:

> Ideally, the developers and I are to work closely together during the design phase... but it typically works out that they gloss over the document or attend a few meetings and get a basic understanding of what we're planning on doing, but never pay attention to the full details. Then they tend to come to me with questions or "Are you crazy? I can't do that!" when it's time for them to put together a timeline for their development assessment. After a few times of close calls, they're beginning to pay more attention to the pencil sketches and overall workflows we put together for them.

I sympathize with this person, but I also believe he or she bears part of the blame. Rather than assume that developers will seek out your design documentation, read all of it, and correctly interpret every detail, you should actively approach the developers and schedule time to sit down and review designs together. And you shouldn't wait until the design phase to do so. For projects in which I'm involved, we often include time during the requirements phase for initial concept sketching. We'll select some of the more nebulous requirements and do upfront design work so that we have a general idea of what the solution is going to entail. I'll review rough pencil sketches with the developers, explain what I'm thinking, and get their input on the technical feasibility of my proposal. This gives the developers a better foundation for creating accurate implementation estimates, and it avoids those contentious debates during implementation in which design vision is compromised to reduce schedule overrun.

Task prioritization

Okay, we can estimate our own tasks, and we can provide developers with information to improve their estimates, but estimates are only one ingredient of project schedules. There's another way designers can contribute to the team's success: task prioritization. In most cases, there will be fewer designers on a team than there will be developers. There's certainly work that developers can do prior to receiving a finished UI design specification, but at some point, they have a dependency on the designer's deliverables. For peak efficiency, you need to be aware of your developers' swim lanes. What feature is each developer working on first? Who is going to need her screen specified first? Are there any tasks you can complete sooner than others? Which features have the most risk, and who is on the critical path to implementing those? You should work closely with your project manager to prioritize your own tasks in such a way that you never have a developer twiddling her thumbs, waiting for you to get around to designing the thing she is supposed to implement next.

Communication

Eventually, it all comes back to communication. A designer must be in constant communication with the rest of the team, sharing design decisions as they happen, rather than waiting to spring a finished masterpiece on them. Effective communication is supported through the use of shared tools.

I put a lot of stock in the tools I use, and I have fought many times to continue using a Mac in an organization that primarily runs Windows. I have a long history with Adobe and the products it has created or acquired. Just as I wouldn't call a plumber and, when he arrived at my house, hand him my wrench and tell him to use it instead of the tools he brought with him, I expect my employer to trust me to select the tools I use. So, I'm the last person that will tell you to stop using the tools that you find most effective for your work, nor would I argue that you have to switch platforms. What I'm preaching is the adoption of additional tools that are used by the developers for the sake of better integration and communication. I've already mentioned task-tracking software. JIRA is web based and therefore cross-platform, so it was easy to pick up. If your team is using something that doesn't have a client on your platform, I suggest requesting for a virtual machine (VM) to be set up that you can access the software on.

Your task management tool is a very important method of communicating with your team. My design tasks will be set up in parallel with development tasks. Let's say there's a system status display feature that we're going to be adding to our product. There are going to be several tasks entered for that one feature:

1. System status display: design
2. System status display: implementation
3. System status display: UI design
4. System status display: UI implementation

There could be others, but this is the minimum, assuming the feature has a UI. The first two tasks are for the developers. Yes, the developers have design tasks too—more on that later. Tasks 3 and 4 are mine. The developer who gets assigned tasks 1 and 2 will "watch" my tasks—that's JIRA's term for subscribing to notifications. Every time I update my task—be it adding a comment, attaching a sketch, or changing its status—the developer will receive an email detailing the update. I'll use the UI design task right from the get-go, recording questions that I need to answer, leaving notes about options I'm considering, and attaching concept sketches. In this way, the developer is constantly in the loop and can add his two cents whenever necessary. I'm not saying this replaces face-to-face communication—it enhances it with full transparency. It also results in a contextual, searchable "paper trail" of any decisions that were made. This is a huge help to the developer as he formulates an estimate.

FIGURE 3.6

Initial concept sketches attached to a UI design task

Another tool that figures prominently in the requirements phase at my company is our development wiki. We use Confluence, another Atlassian product. It began as a place for the developers to document their architectural designs, but quickly grew to contain all of the information we need to share. Each project gets its own space. When we receive an FRD from a client, it's entered into the wiki. From that point on, as the requirements are clarified and modified, the wiki keeps track of the changes. We record questions that we want to pose to the customer, and then we log the answers. All of the information I gather from my research is filed there as well, making it available to the entire team. Of course, we all subscribe to the project, so we all receive email notification when a page is added or updated. Yes, it can create a lot of email noise, but the peripheral awareness is well worth it. I set up rules in my email application that dump notifications from JIRA and Confluence into specific folders. That way, they don't clog up my inbox, and I can quickly peruse them, checking for relevant items, when I'm ready for a status update.

Maybe your developers are using a wiki too, or maybe they aren't. Your company may employ a specialized requirements-tracking tool for this purpose. We have begun evaluating such tools to support distributed teams. My purpose here isn't to dictate a set of tools that you should be using. Rather, I'm urging you to find out what tools your developers are using and figure out how you can hook into them. Communication is happening through these tools, and you need to be in the loop. When you're all sharing the same tools, you'll be sharing your thoughts and ideas; you'll be sharing your questions and answers; you'll be sharing your problems and solutions.

There will be a shared understanding of the requirements, goals, and strategies that shape the project—both technical and experiential. That's a big win for the team, and if you'll pardon a little bit of sneaky selfishness, it's a huge win for designers. These tools allow us to extend our influence, spreading awareness of UX concerns among all team members in a subtle, yet irresistible, fashion.

It may be the case that your team isn't using these types of tools. Of the survey respondents, 15% claimed that nobody at their company was using issue-tracking software. If you find yourself in such a situation, I suggest approaching it as an opportunity to make a positive impact on your team's effectiveness. Talk to the senior developers and project managers about the process inefficiencies they're currently dealing with and suggest trying a tool that will help address their issues. It may not even take a financial investment to start incorporating project management tools. Inexpensive hosting solutions, like Codebase and Trello, can get your team up and running quickly.

FIGURE 3.7

Trello sample project board

Trello is a general-use, online organization and collaboration tool from Fog Creek Software. With it, you can create and assign tasks with deadlines and notifications. It provides basic capabilities, such as commenting, file attachments, and checklists, and it has apps on the major mobile platforms. It's free, so it is a great way to get your feet wet.

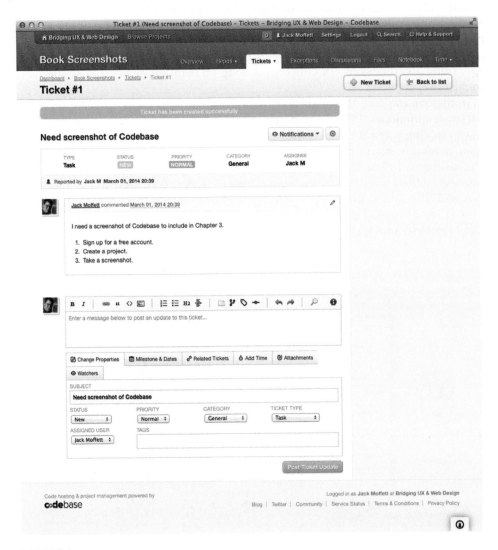

FIGURE 3.8

Codebase ticket

Codebase, as the name implies, is specifically targeted at software development. The service hosts code repositories (which I'll go over in Chapter 5) and provides a suite of tools for project management, including issue tracking, time tracking, project notebooks (like a wiki), and discussions. Codebase also offers a free, if limited, account. It's enough for you to try out on your next project. Not only can you potentially improve your team's process, but I imagine you'll earn some serious bonus points doing it.

DESIGN

The design phase is the part of the project in which the details of the UI are determined and specified. If you're an interaction designer, this is likely the phase with which you most identify. You may be sketching, creating wireframes, generating pixel-perfect mockups, and prototyping by various methods. These activities are well understood, and I'm going to make the assumption that I don't have to explain the common activities of designers during the design phase any further. Instead, I'd like to focus on two things: the activities of our developer friends and design documentation.

Code design

You'll recall the "system status display: design" task that I stated was a developer task. The developers have a design phase also, and it can happen in parallel with the designer's activities. During design, developers will be planning the architecture of the application. How is the functionality organized into objects, calls, variables, and other technical mumbo-jumbo such that the application can function efficiently and without errors? What patterns will be employed? What parts of the code are going to be componentized for reuse? What services should be made available? This is where some of that preliminary UI design work is going to be helpful to them, and you should keep the communication channels open.

Assuming you have a good working relationship with your developers, you should expect frequent interruptions as they gather the details to make decisions about their designs. Welcome these interruptions. If you become annoyed and give the impression that the developers are bothering you—that you're too busy to care about their problems—they may just stop asking, and that's the path to the dark side. Regardless of how much work you have to do to meet your deadline, it'll all be for naught if the developers make uninformed decisions that preclude the interactivity you're envisioning. A fair amount of negotiation may have to happen as they fully realize the implications of your initial concepts. You may end up making significant changes or reversing direction on certain issues, and that's okay. Remain flexible, make smart concessions, and pick your battles. Remember my advice from Chapter 2, and you'll come out smelling… well, not so much like roses—maybe more like pizza and Mountain Dew.

If your team is doing contract work for a customer, you're likely going to have a design review before implementation begins. You'll be presenting your UI designs for approval, and the developers will be presenting their design as well. I often offer my graphic design skills to the developers for key architectural diagrams that we feel are especially important for the customer to understand. I've created state change diagrams and data flow diagrams for them that more effectively communicate the issues we're dealing with, such as race conditions, than UML diagrams do and help them understand the options we present and our recommended solutions. If you or other members of your team are visual designers, I recommend planning some time for such work. After all, it's a team effort, and improving the developers' part of the presentation is going to benefit everyone.

Documentation

If you're a devotee of Lean UX or Agile, you may not have much use for documentation. We may just have to agree to disagree, but please hear me out. Even if you consider a design specification document to be the ultimate evil, there might be something here you'll find beneficial. Given the work I do and the customers I do it for, documentation is a necessity. I have to document the UI design so that it can be communicated to and understood by our customers. I have to document UI behaviors so that they'll be correctly implemented by our developers and validated by our testers. I have to document my own decisions so that, six months from now, when a question is raised about a particular function, and I'm neck-deep in a different project, I can explain what issues were raised, what options were considered, and what outcome was reached. I don't know about you, but after working through multiple iterations, I sometimes have trouble remembering what we ended up with, let alone how we got there. I'm aware, however, that a lot of organizations generate too much documentation that's never referenced; hence the backlash against it. I caution you not to throw the baby out with the bathwater. My slogan is "documentation in moderation."

The key is to design your documentation for its intended audience. If you have to communicate your design to the customer, you don't need to create a document that details the UI at a granularity needed to implement it. You're likely going to want something that presents the design from a task-based perspective. There may be a fair amount of narrative.

On the other hand, in a specification document intended for a developer, you need something that's more concise and easily referenced. While the developers will benefit from understanding the task flows, they shouldn't have to search through a narrative explaining how the user works through a sequence of steps to find out what state the UI should be in when a particular radio button is clicked. Here are a few basic guidelines for creating documentation that developers will not only use, but will come to depend on:

- *Design documentation to be a reference tool.* Don't write your documentation with the expectation that it'll be read start-to-finish. Treat it as a reference that the developer will consult as needed. Any given developer is only going to need certain parts of it. Number your pages. Use clear section headings. Create a table of contents. Organize it in a way that makes sense for the project team, rather than for the customer or the users. This may mean that functions are documented based on location, rather than in task order.

- *Always reference the requirements.* If your team is correctly using tools like JIRA to track requirements, feature requests, bugs, and the like, there

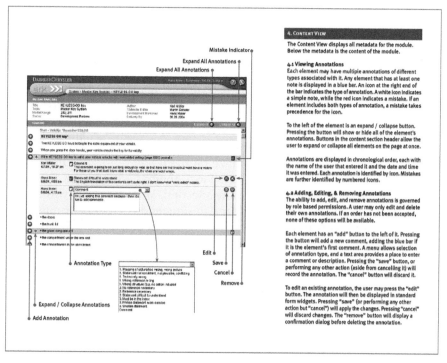

FIGURE 3.9

This is a document explaining a UI design to a customer. The labels are descriptive, rather than specifications, pointing out features mentioned in the heavy narrative to the right of the screen mockup.

are going to be reference numbers. Use them in your documentation. Traceability between project documents, both the team's and the customer's, helps ensure that nothing is missed or lost.

- *Be concise and explicit in your explanations.* A design specification shouldn't be an exercise in creative writing; it's a set of instructions that are to be followed. Furthermore, it shouldn't leave room for interpretation. Consider the following description: "When the user clicks delete, a confirmation dialog opens and asks them if they are sure they want to delete the item. If they press 'Yes,' close the dialog and remove the item from the list. If they press 'No,' close the dialog without deleting the item." This explanation may be understandable, but it contains a lot of superfluous verbiage while leaving out important details. We can assume that it's "the user" who is clicking the button. We can also assume that the developer understands what a delete confirmation dialog is and shouldn't have to explain how one works every time it's invoked. The description doesn't state how the software knows which item is to be deleted, and it doesn't specify that it's referring to a delete button, rather than a link or other control. Here's a better way to specify the interaction: "When Delete button is pressed, display confirmation, then remove selected item." The sentence wouldn't score you an A in your high school English class, but that's not its purpose. It succinctly and accurately describes the interaction in a minimal number of words. It'll take some practice to train yourself to write this way, but eventually, you'll do it naturally, and it'll save time both in the writing and reading.

- *Label screens effectively.* It goes without saying that your documentation should include sketches, mockups, or screenshots (depending on what you're documenting), but to capitalize on the utility of the document, you should label your screens effectively. First, number your figures for easy reference during phone conversations. Second, label elements within the screens that are being specified. Many designers drop letters or numbers onto their screens with corresponding references in the text. This turns your UI into a puzzle that must be deciphered. I prefer to draw arrows to

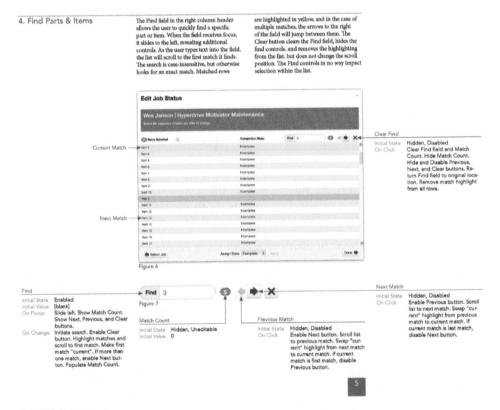

FIGURE 3.10

Sample page from a specification document

the elements that are being specified, labeling them directly and providing the essential information about each one. This is extremely useful as a reference, because the developers don't have to peruse a paragraph trying to find the one piece of information they need. Try to avoid diagonal lines. Keeping your lines vertical and horizontal will result in a more orderly display. If you must use diagonal lines, try to maintain a consistent angle. Also, avoid crossing lines. Use a contrasting color that isn't prevalent in your screens (e.g., bright red) so that they stand out. Using a grid to align information around an image will keep your page organized and easily scannable. Following all of these suggestions will make it quick and easy for developers to get what they need out of your screens.

- *Be thorough.* Make sure you include all of the necessary details. Forms for entering information are common in most software, and while they may not be the hardest part to design, they're often the most tedious to document. Every field, menu, and checkbox has a slew of potential attributes. What is its initial state? Is it prefilled? Does it validate its content? Is it required? Does it have any behavior on focus? On change? On blur? Good design documentation doesn't leave a developer guessing.

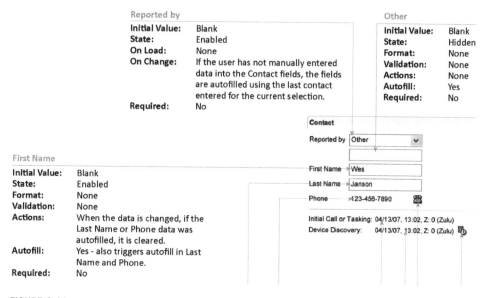

FIGURE 3.11

Example of form element specification

- *Be consistent.* Every specification document you deliver to your developers should follow the same conventions. This isn't to say you can't make improvements, but you won't improve productivity if the developers have to relearn how to use your documents every time you deliver one. Your organization should develop templates for each type of document you use, and every designer should use them. Consider each document type to be a tool that must be learned, utilized, and maintained. Design documentation should be reviewed for quality, completeness, and adherence to standards just as you critique UI designs.

Interesting Moments Grid

An excellent example of documentation that has been designed specifically for use by developers is the Interesting Moments Grid (IMG). Invented by Bill Scott at Yahoo!, the grid breaks down complex interactions into their individual actors and steps, clearly representing each change in state that occurs. The columns of the grid represent the events that occur during an interaction in order from left to right. Every actor in the interaction is given a row in the grid. For example, Figure 3.12 shows a multiselect widget documented in an IMG.

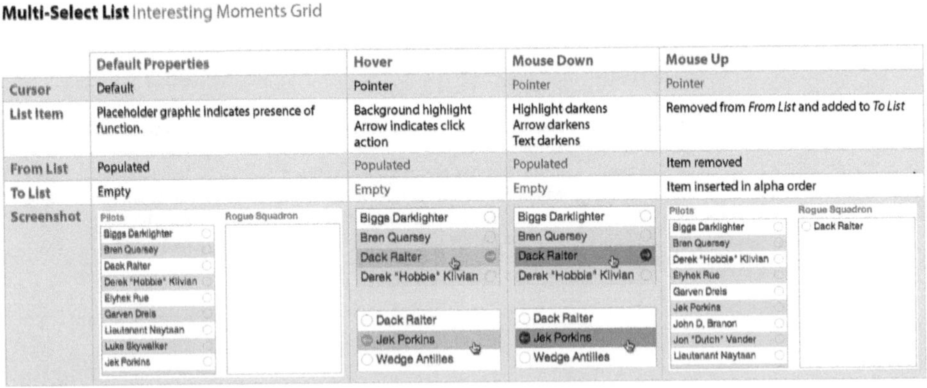

Multi-Select List Interesting Moments Grid

	Default Properties	Hover	Mouse Down	Mouse Up
Cursor	Default	Pointer	Pointer	Pointer
List Item	Placeholder graphic indicates presence of function.	Background highlight Arrow indicates click action	Highlight darkens Arrow darkens Text darkens	Removed from *From List* and added to *To List*
From List	Populated	Populated	Populated	Item removed
To List	Empty	Empty	Empty	Item inserted in alpha order
Screenshot				

FIGURE 3.12

Interesting Moments Grid

As you can see, the grid makes every attribute of the interaction immediately apparent. It's easy to create (you could even do it in Excel—I wouldn't, but you could), and it enforces a level of rigor, in that an empty cell indicates that something may be missing. After introducing the grid to my developers, they encouraged me to indicate state in every cell, even if it hasn't changed, as that way, it's apparent that nothing has been left out. I decided to use text color to indicate when changes in state happen. For more on the IMG, see Bill Scott's slide deck, *Designing for Interesting Moments (http://www.slideshare.net/ billwscott/designing-interesting-moments),* and Jared Spool's article, *Capturing the Interesting Moments (http://www.uie.com/articles/interesting_moments).*

Minimum required documentation

While I obviously disagree with Lean UX proponents who have declared design specification documents to be worthless, I'll agree that we should reduce documentation to what is essential. This is right in line with the primary goal of this book: to get designers to implement their designs. You see, if you're the one who will be turning your screen mockups into HTML and CSS, then there's a lot less specification for you to do. You know what color an element is going to be. You know how much spacing to put between elements and what font size to use. You know what is supposed to happen when the cursor hovers over a button. Since you already know all of those things, there's no need for you to include them in your specification document. I only document that which a developer will have to implement or the customer has to approve. Button hover states are a detail that the customer typically isn't going to think about (unless they notice that they are missing) and that I'll be creating with CSS—no developer needed. I never document hover states unless they're communicating something more than that a button is clickable.

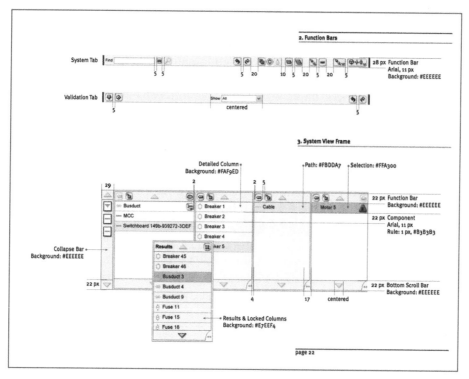

FIGURE 3.13

This page is from a UI design specification document for an application that was to be implemented in Eclipse RCP. Nothing on the page would be necessary if the UI were implemented in HTML and CSS.

IMPLEMENTATION

> I get most frustrated when, after providing a pixel-perfect mockup, I see the finished implementation during the testing phase, and it's drastically different than what I spec'd (fonts, colors, sizes, spacing, alignment, positioning, etc.).

This comment, shared by one of the survey participants, illustrates exactly why every designer working on software should be breaking down the door to participate during the implementation phase of a project. As I explained in Chapter 2, we can't expect the developers, who haven't had the visual or experiential training that we have, nor possess our sensibilities, to pick up on every nuance of a mockup or prototype. Excuse my bluntness, but if you're handing off your design to a developer and not seeing anything until the testing phase, you're doing it wrong.

It's vital for designers to remain involved throughout the entire development process, including implementation. Delivering a design specification to the developers is a major milestone, certainly, but it isn't the end of your work. As the developers are implementing the UI, there will be issues that arise requiring additional decisions and further tradeoffs. Designers should keep tabs on the progress the developers are making, patiently pointing out any discrepancies and explaining how to correct them. If you're using a task-tracking tool, you can watch the developers' implementation tasks to receive notifications about their progress. Developers will typically record comments about challenges they're facing and options they're considering. You can stay abreast of potential changes and contribute to the dialog when you have relevant input.

Communication is very important, but it's only going to get you so far. If you truly want to remain in control of the user experience, and I'm adamant that you should, then you should be implementing the UI. And that brings us to the million-dollar question, described by Jared Spool in his article *"Why the Valley Wants Designers That Can Code"*:

> If you're in a room filled with designers, bring up the topic of whether it's valuable for a designer to also code. Immediately, the room will divide faster than Moses split the Red Sea. One side will tell you coding is an essential skill, while the other will vehemently argue how it dilutes the designer's value.

Jared Spool is proven correct by the IxDA LinkedIn group discussion (*http://goo.gl/Y3XdVi*) that raged for over a year with 480 comments, as well as more recent debates like this one, which occurred as a disparate series of blog posts:

- *"Unicorn, Shmunicorn—Be a Pegasus,"* by Wayne Greenwood: *http://www.waynegreenwood.com/unicorn-shmunicorn-be-a-pegasus/.*

- *"'Designers Shouldn't Code' Is the Wrong Answer to the Right Question,"* by Joshua Seiden: *http://joshuaseiden.com/blog/2013/08/designers-shouldnt-code-is-the-wrong-answer-to-the-right-question/.*

- *"Thoughts on Code, Programming, Design, Production, Development, Technology, and Oh! Design,"* by Dave Malouf: *http://davemalouf. com/?p=2390.*

- *"Design, Production, and Craft—What Do Designers Make?"* by Matt Nish-Lapidus: *http://ideas.normative.com/practice/design-production-and-craft-what-do-designers-make.*

Do designers need to code? There are plenty of opinions and convincing arguments both for and against. I certainly know many very talented designers who don't know how to code who are extremely successful, so apparently designers don't *need* to code. My own conviction is that this is the wrong question altogether. Rather than asking whether we need to code, we should be asking, "Will learning to code make me a better designer?" The answer to that question is going to vary from person to person, depending greatly on context: the type of work you do, the type of firm you work for, the makeup of your team, and what you want to do in the future.

I surveyed the LinkedIn discussion, and all of the arguments against designers learning to code can be summarized in the following three perceived drawbacks.

Drawback 1: If you know how to code, you'll be tasked with coding instead of designing

Jennifer Tidwell, author of *Designing Interfaces: Patterns for Effective Interaction*, wrote in a post on her blog, "I found that when I tried to be both a designer and engineer/coder, I ended up doing a lot more engineering and a lot less design than I wanted to do. I think part of the problem is that engineering skills are, in the end, valued more than design skills" (*http://designinginterfaces.com/2011/06/01/designers-that-code-a-response-to-jared-spool/*). There's a real danger here, depending on the company you work for. If your company doesn't value design, and they know that they can use you as another developer, then you may find yourself in the picture Jennifer paints. Of course, that will likely be one of many challenges you face. In that situation, you have three choices: live with it, try to change it, or leave for greener pastures. If your company truly values design, then your project schedules will be built with time for design. Tools like Microsoft Project plot out tasks in a Gantt chart, visualizing who each task is assigned to and dependencies on tasks assigned to others. If the designer is tasked with both design tasks and implementation tasks, the schedule will reflect it by pushing the implementation tasks out past the end of the design tasks. This is one reason accurate estimates are so important.

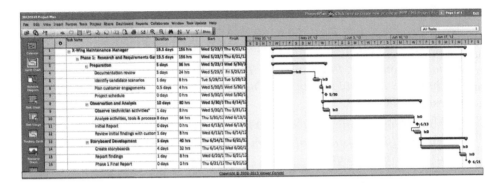

FIGURE 3.14

Gantt chart

Now, some designers see coding as a chore. They don't want to code because they don't enjoy it, and that's okay. As I already said, there are plenty of places for designers to work without having to do a lick of code. But don't cite implementation tasking as a drawback just because you don't want to do it. I enjoy implementing my designs. I get great satisfaction from implementing an interaction to look and behave exactly the way I intend it to, knowing that it'll improve the user experience. As you'll see in the latter half of this book, I also take great satisfaction from writing efficient, maintainable code. That takes nothing away from my enjoyment of design—rather, it enhances it. If I had to choose between performing only design activities and implementation, I would choose design in a heartbeat, but I don't have to choose. I can do both, and everybody benefits.

Drawback 2: If you know how to code, you'll limit your creativity due to the known difficulty of implementation

This is a surprisingly common argument, albeit a weak one. The good news is that this one is completely in your control. Are you lazy? Are you a sub-par designer who isn't passionate about delivering the best experience possible to your users? No, I didn't think so. That type of person probably wouldn't care enough to pick up a copy of this book, let alone read this much of it. I expect you have enough self-discipline to explore possibilities that you may not know how to implement, but can learn, while tempering your designs to avoid what you know to be technically infeasible. Don't forget Will Jameson from Chapter 2. He'll be happy to help you with any feasibility questions you have. I really don't worry too much about implementation while I'm designing. Sure, I may realize that I don't know offhand how to implement what I'm sketching, but rather than fixate on that, I shrug it off as a bridge to cross later. I have confidence that I and my team can figure something out. If we can't, I'll revise the design.

Drawback 3: You'll marginalize your design skills to add coding skills

This perceived drawback also goes by the label "Jack of all trades—master of none." The basic idea here is that there's only so much time to learn everything you need to know to be a designer. If you use some of that time to learn to program, you'll have missed out on some of the design skills. You may be a good designer and a lousy developer, but you'll never be a great designer, and you can't be good at both. In that case, so the argument goes, you're better off being a great designer and leaving code to others. People who make this claim are awfully short-sighted. There are too many variables to pin down exactly how long an average career is, but let's say you spend 4 years as an undergraduate, take 2 years to get a master's degree at some point, and retire at 65 years old. That's going to give you about 40 years working in the field, which is a long time, and I hope you aren't planning to rest on your laurels for half of it. While writing this very chapter, I completed my fifteenth year as a professional interaction designer. I've collected advanced skills in visual design, interaction design, and front-end web development. You can bet I'm not going to stop learning now. I'm hoping that my best work is yet to be done.

Of course, you have to start somewhere. You can't learn everything all at once and expect to excel at everything. I started with visual design, earning a bachelor's degree in graphic design. Then I went to graduate school for a master's degree in interaction design. I have, of course, continued to develop both sets of skills during my employment, but over the course of those 15 years, I've also learned how to write HTML and CSS well enough to contribute to the production code base. I've specifically focused on that area in the past few years. There have been articles written in the past about the T-shaped designer (see *http://www.core77.com/back2work/2009/09/on_being_tshaped. asp*). The vertical stem of the T represents deep expertise in one specialty (like interaction design or information architecture). The cross bar, then, represents shallower knowledge in adjacent areas (e.g., visual design or coding) that complement one's specialty, rounding out his or her skill set.

It's a good model for a junior designer, but why stop at T? Once you're T-shaped, deepen one of those adjacent areas to become n-shaped. Then, deepen a third to become m-shaped. The order isn't necessarily important, but I'd like to give you some advice here as well. From my own experience, and granted, my own bias, I recommend improving your visual design skills before moving on to code. Visual design and communication skills will be more beneficial to you as a UX professional than coding skills, and you should be able to visualize a UI design (not just wireframe it) before implementing it. I should also point out that there are certainly more potential ingredients for designer soup than the ones I have. Writing, industrial design, cognitive psychology, anthropology, library science, and business are all areas that you could potentially benefit from. Ultimately, you'll have to decide where your interests lie and what skills you think will make you the best designer for your situation.

Ah, yes, I had mentioned context. Your context is extremely important. I have been working in a small software development firm. During most of my time there, I have been the only interaction designer. We don't have a front-end developer, one who would specialize in HTML, CSS, JavaScript, and so forth without doing back-end server work. As such, I have always been responsible for both the visual and interaction design of our products, and it didn't take me long to surpass our developers in my knowledge of HTML and CSS. I still leave the JavaScript to them. I know enough to edit it if I want small changes made, but I can't write it from scratch. That's where we have found a natural equilibrium of knowledge, interest, and time on task. Perhaps I'll learn more JavaScript in the future, or it may make sense to leave that division as it is and pursue other skills instead.

That's my context, but, as the survey results in Chapter 1 illustrated, there are many other contexts. There are a lot of firms that employ graphic designers and interaction designers as completely separate roles. Interaction designers create wireframes and collaborate with graphic designers who are responsible for the visual design. Likewise, there are many firms that employ front-end developers. If I were working in such a firm, perhaps I'd never have learned the implementation skill set I now have. You'll have to decide for yourself whether coding is something you'll find useful in your practice as a designer. Jared Spool, in his article *"Why the Valley Wants Designers That Can Code,"* has some wisdom to share on this matter (emphasis added):

Coding and designing are collections of skills. What we've learned is teams with a better distribution of skills, *not segmented by roles,* produce better results.

Don't just think about your current position and current company when deciding whether or not learning to code is for you. Consider where you'd like to go in your career. Coding is a skill set that's going to make you more capable of practicing design in a wider variety of contexts. It'll make you more valuable and more attractive in most situations. The benefits far outweigh the perceived drawbacks I just refuted.

Also drawn from the LinkedIn discussion from which I culled the perceived drawbacks, here are the perceived benefits of learning to code.

Benefit 1: Calling BS on coders

Have you ever been in a situation where a developer was telling you that your design couldn't be implemented, and you thought they were lying (or at least wrong), but didn't have enough knowledge to call their bluff? It's unfortunate, but it does happen. A lot of designers claim this particular benefit, but I'm not so sure. This is a very combative stance to take, and if you read Chapter 2, you know how I feel about designer–developer relationships. If you're in a work environment filled with mistrust, learning to code for this benefit is wasted effort. There are bigger problems that you should be seeking solutions to, rather than perpetuating a divisive atmosphere by throwing accusations, provable or not.

Benefit 2: Respect and credibility

Also cited by many designers, apparently developers will respect you more if you can code. I can see why this might be true, but I believe this, too, a false benefit. In a properly functioning team, people will respect other people for their skill, talent, professionalism, leadership, dedication, and positive attitude, regardless of their particular skill set. I want the developers I work with to respect me as an outstanding designer first and foremost. That comes from working together on projects and sharing the failures, the late nights, the triumphs, and the successful rollouts. It comes from a learned appreciation for my contributions over time. My coding ability may factor into it, but it's only a small part. I gained the respect of my coworkers long before I was able to check my code into Subversion.

Benefit 3: Speaking their language

This may well be the most cited benefit of learning to code. Certainly, it's easier to communicate with developers when we can understand their terminology. It helps even more to understand their concerns and challenges. That said, I don't believe it's necessary to learn to code to develop that understanding. You can learn this simply by talking with developers, asking them questions, and listening to them. You learn how to speak their language by caring enough to pay attention. What you learn from coding is much more detailed, and while it'll undoubtedly give you a better appreciation of what they do, this alone isn't a good reason to learn how to code.

Benefit 4: Knowledge of capabilities and difficulty of implementation

This is the flip side of drawback 2. By knowing how to code, you'll have a better understanding of what can and can't be done, what is hard or easy to do, and what takes more or less time. This may or may not be true. Just because I understand front-end web development doesn't mean I have any sense of the impacts my design will have on the back-end database. Much like benefit 3, you don't necessarily have to know how to code to understand technical feasibility.

Benefit 5: Prototyping

There are many different ways to create prototypes. There are prototyping tools, such as Axure and Balsamiq, that allow you to build interactive prototypes without knowing how to code. You can use presentation software, such as Apple's Keynote or Microsoft PowerPoint. Tools like these can get you a long way down the road, and in many cases, they're sufficient to get the answers you need. However, the ability to prototype using the same technology that will be used in implementation does have additional benefits. It's often easier to create behaviors with the native technology than to reproduce them with a different technology. For example, once you understand how to create a scrolling pane with the rubber-band effect in an iPhone app, I'm sure it's much easier to do it that way than to mimic the rubber-band effect in Adobe After Effects, and then you can actually experience using it on the target device rather than watching it. Furthermore, when you prototype with the actual technology, you know that what you see is what you get. It's not possible to prototype something that's impossible to build. And, of course, there's the potential to turn your prototype into the actual software, although that's usually not the goal of a prototype. Depending on your circumstances, there may be reason enough to learn to code for purposes of prototyping.

Benefit 6: Reduced documentation

I've already discussed this in the context of the design phase, so I'll only mention it here briefly. There are definite time savings when you can implement the specifics of a UI rather than documenting them for somebody else.

Benefit 7: Control

Of all the potential benefits to learning to code, control is the one that seals the deal. When you're able to implement your designs, you're in almost complete control of the outcome. Rather than fretting over the discrepancies that occur when well-meaning developers mishandle your design, you can get things right the first time. If you see a mistake made by you or by someone else, you can fix it without having to bother a developer about it. When the product goes out the door, you know that it's what you made it. I can take care of every little detail that fits into my estimated schedule, and that's going to make a big difference in the final product. That should be enough to get most designers interested. It was enough for Matt Nish-Lapidus at Normative, who stated,

> ...we're instituting a new professional development program here at Normative. For the next few months, we're all taking an hour a day to dig into front-end web and mobile code. We're going to learn to bring our ideas to life and start designing all the details that are often missed when we just make pictures.

To code or not to code?

I've clearly laid out the pros and cons; now it's up to you. Does it make sense for you to spend some time honing your coding skills? Actually, this isn't an all-or-nothing question. Learning to code doesn't have to mean becoming competent enough to deliver production-ready code. There are many directions it can take, and it's going to depend greatly on your context. The following questions can help you decide.

- *What's your company's technology stack?* Spending a lot of time learning CSS is less likely to help you if your company primarily builds enterprise desktop applications in C++. You need to figure out what code you should learn. If you do a lot of web- and browser-based work, you should definitely start by getting a good grasp of HTML and CSS. Part II of this book can help you with that. It'd also be beneficial, once you're comfortable, to add some knowledge of JavaScript, especially through the use of a framework like jQuery (see Chapter 9). A library such as Bootstrap will also be helpful. On the other hand, your firm may have invested heavily in Ruby on Rails or .NET, in which case, knowledge of those platforms may serve you better. If you're developing native, mobile applications, there are other libraries, tools, frameworks, etc. that would be of greater use.

- *What is your team makeup?* Are you working with a bunch of back-end Java developers who only have a basic understanding of CSS? In that situation, you're going to reap great rewards for doubling-down and growing your implementation skills. Do you have full-on front-end developers on your team? If so, your organization may not want you spending time on production code at all. If that's the case, you're probably looking for just enough know-how to prototype your ideas and play around with new technologies. That's a lot less daunting of a hill to climb. Knowing enough to be able to copy snippets of code off the web and paste them into your pages will enable you to experience interactions that you wouldn't otherwise and demonstrate them to your developers.

- *What is your destiny?* The fact that you're in your current position with your current company working on its current products doesn't necessarily mean that's where you want to be or what you want to be working on five years from now. Educating yourself on coding is certainly something that can deliver immediate benefits, but you should be planning for the future. What do you want to be able to put on your résumé? What position do you wish to be able to apply to? What platforms do you hope to design for?

Whatever your decision may be, I hope this book helps you develop effective relationships and work practices with your development team. We have one more phase to address in the collaboration life cycle, after which, the remaining chapters will focus on production-ready HTML and CSS.

TESTING AND EVALUATION

At the end of the implementation phase, a product must be tested against the design to ensure it works as intended. Hopefully you'll be pursuing some form of usability evaluation to see if the working version is as easy to use as you thought it'd be. At the same time, the developers will be carrying out their functional testing.

Not to be confused with usability testing, functional testing is the phase in which the development team tests their implementation to make sure it works correctly. The team writes test cases, explaining the steps one should go through to thoroughly test a particular function and what should happen if it functions properly. Whenever there's a discrepancy, a bug gets logged. Your design specification is a great reference when writing those test cases, so that's one way you can assist the team, but there's an even better way. As it turns out, designers make outstanding testers. We're detail-oriented, so we notice everything. In addition, we use the system more like a user would, so we may run into issues that test cases don't bring to light. Many such issues may not even be functional bugs, per se, but usability bugs. If we can catch some of these, log them as bugs, and get them fixed before formal user testing, so much the better. And then there's the fact that we should know better than anyone how the thing is supposed to work. We're the ones who designed it.

Just as designers can participate in functional testing, consider engaging some of your developers in user testing, especially field trials. The experience will give them a better appreciation of the users' concerns. I've seen developers I work with develop true empathy for the people who are required to use our software. It's one thing for you to tell the developers that the users had problems with this or needed that, but it'll be even more impactful if one of their own is as adamant about usability concerns as you are.

And that brings us full circle. The collaboration life cycle is complete. The designer and developer fist-bump as the customer lauds them for another on-schedule, underbudget release of intuitive, bug-free software goodness. Alright, I can't promise all that, but the fist-bump... that's genuine.

PART II

Sitting in the Driver's Seat

If designers aren't participating in implementation, they are giving up control of the user experience. All of the time and effort put into specifying and prototyping the microinteractions of a product may be for naught if you aren't there to see it through. Any amount of involvement is going to help, but to maximize one's influence, a designer should be hands-on, implementing as much of the UI as he or she is capable of. According to a recent survey of 963 user experience professionals conducted by Nielsen Norman Group, 94% of us have worked on websites and web applications (http://www.nngroup.com /articles/ux-career-advice/). We are fortunate that the languages used in front-end web development are relatively easy to learn. Through competency, and eventually mastery, we can sit in the driver's seat, steering the user experience of our products through implementation, safely circumnavigating obstacles, and ensuring faithful interpretation of our intent. Buckle your seatbelt; we're going for a drive.

Why HTML and CSS?

The title of the book aside, so far I've been trying to refer to code generically. This may have left you chomping at the bit to say something like, "My company writes desktop applications. Surely, you don't expect me to learn C++." Or, maybe you've been silently fuming, "But writing HTML and CSS isn't *real* coding." Yes, there's a big difference between front-end scripting languages and compiled, back-end code. Front-end languages are easier to learn, quicker to work with, and they deal specifically with the user interface—its appearance and behavior—which is what we care about the most.

Most of the software I've worked on has been browser-based. On the few occasions that I worked on desktop applications, I wasn't implementing the UI myself. I don't expect designers to become software engineers, but I do believe that we should learn enough to be able to contribute our expertise as directly as possible. If I were to work on a desktop application today, I'd work with the developers to find a way that I could have more direct influence over the UI, even if it meant that I had to learn some of whatever language was employed.

The topic of designers learning to code came up during an IxDA Pittsburgh panel discussion. Francisco Souki, a game designer at Schell Games, explained to us that in game development, the designers aren't expected to know how to program the games. The languages used and code produced are very complex. The developers would never let one of the designers touch the production code. However, the game designers have to be able to manipulate behaviors in the live game and see the effects in real time. Balancing game mechanics is tricky business, and working things out on paper will only get you so far. So, how can the game designers do this if they aren't allowed to touch the code?

It'd be terribly inefficient to have a game designer looking over the developer's shoulder saying, "Okay, let's have him move just a little faster, and can we reduce the jump height a tiny bit?" Francisco described tools that the developers build for the express purposes of designers tweaking gameplay.

The tools are basically forms with labeled fields containing numeric variables for attributes such as speed, hit points, power, cool down, and the like. The designer can manipulate the values while running the game to see their effects. The tools take the bits out of the code that the designers care about and present them in a format understandable by the designer. This is exactly what a Cascading Style Sheet is. CSS takes the values that we care about controlling in a page and presents them to us using language we can understand in a format that's easy for us to manipulate.

HTML and CSS are at a perfect level of difficulty and control for interaction designers. Structuring a page in HTML is very similar to creating wireframes, and CSS speaks our language: position, dimension, color, type. Even if you're designing UIs for non-web platforms, such as native mobile applications or traditional desktop applications, HTML can be a very powerful prototyping tool. More than that, HTML can be the perfect gateway to programming for those platforms. Ask any developer, and she or he will tell you that once you've learned one language, it's easier to learn another. It just so happens that a lot of designers are primarily developing for the web: 88% of the survey respondents claimed proficiency in HTML, 79% use CSS, only 36% claimed to use JavaScript competently versus 30% for jQuery, PHP had 25%, and everything fell off the cliff after that. Perhaps it's no surprise that every one of the 24% of respondents who work with production code claim competence in both HTML and CSS. All but one use JavaScript (including jQuery).

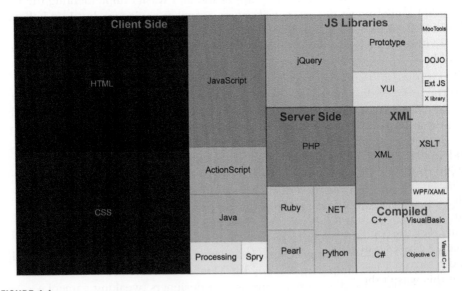

FIGURE 4.1

Treemap of language/library proficiency
You can interact with this visualization on IBM's Many Eyes website: *http://www-958.ibm.com/v/137864*.

Chances are, you already have basic knowledge of HTML and CSS. If you don't, I recommend picking up a few introductory books before continuing this one. I highly recommend *CSS 3 for Web Designers* by Dan Cederholm. My purpose for the second half of this book isn't to teach basics, but to prepare you to contribute production code. While most web designers know how to write HTML and CSS, they don't do so with the discipline necessary to produce elegant code that improves performance and is easy to maintain. Just as a good UI is designed to be usable by the people using the software, the code has to be designed to be usable by the development team.

SHARE THE HTML, OWN THE STYLE SHEET

Everyone touches the HTML. The developers will have to chop it up and jam it into server-side templates. They'll be inserting JavaScript calls all over the place, and they have to ensure that they have unique IDs on all of the important elements. With this in mind, you should design the HTML to be shared.

Comments

The first lesson in sharing code comes directly from the developers' playbook. Comment your code. Even if you're only creating mockups for developers to copy and paste out of, comments are a great way to explain your intent within the context that the developers need it. I use comments to explain to the developers exactly what classes are available to change the state of an element, what elements to place them on, and under what conditions. Comments can be used to identify what content in a page is dynamic and should be generated by JavaScript. And, of course, comments are handy for identifying sections of code as areas of the UI.

Silly designer, IDs are for devs

Generally, I try not to use IDs in my CSS. If I don't include IDs in selectors, then I have no dependencies on them, and the developers are free to use them without worrying about messing up the styling of elements. Occasionally, I'll have to use an ID, especially when integrating a third-party component, but given the choice, I always use classes. The classes, then, I consider to be mine. I work with the expectation that the developers will not add, remove, or change classes without asking me first. I assume that I can safely add, change, and remove classes without messing up the JavaScript. There have been times that this wasn't the case—when JavaScript was looking for a class as a way to identify a particular element state. This is certainly a valid thing to do, and I'll be explaining the use of state classes in Chapter 7, but in most cases, it makes things easier to let the developers control the IDs and the designers own the classes.

Just say "No!" to inline styles

All styles should be written in style sheets and applied via classes. Hopefully, you already understand that inline styles take precedence over those in style sheets, as do styles defined in the `<head>`. Defining styles within the HTML will limit your ability to change them under different conditions, and one of your goals should be to retain as much flexibility as possible. Your developers may not have this understanding. I've found that developers are very fond of having their JavaScript write `style="display: none;"` directly into the page when they need to hide an element. If your developers share this habit, my first recommendation is to create a style expressly for this purpose:

```
.hidden {
    display: none;
}
```

Train your developers to add the `hidden` class to elements, rather than writing inline styles. Work with your team to enforce a strict ban on inline styles. There are cases where the developers will need to control an element dynamically—say to size an object on the page like a progress bar—and those cases will indeed require inline styles. But for most uses of inline styles, you should be able to create a simple solution like the preceding one. This will allow you to override these classes with greater specificity in your selectors when necessary. Of course, many of these cases are better served by a well-designed system of state classes, but as I said, we'll get to that in Chapter 7.

Own the CSS

The style sheet should be wholly owned by the designers. Developers don't have the visual design chops to fine-tune the CSS, and as we went over earlier, that typically isn't what they want to spend their time doing. CSS is really written for graphic designers, utilizing picas, ems, and points. It provides quite a lot of typographic control, which is a good thing, since most of what you're working with on screen—from content, to navigation, to input forms—is text. For those of you without a graphic design background, might I suggest reading up a bit on typography basics? Ellen Lupton's *Thinking with Type* would give you a solid foundation for understanding how CSS measurements work and why you'd want to use anything other than a pixel. But, I digress. The point is, CSS is made for designers, and we're suited to working with that which CSS controls. It's a match made in heaven, or at least in the W3C. It makes sense, then, for the designers to take responsibility for maintaining the style sheets, as well as the processes surrounding them.

That's not to say that others aren't allowed to touch the CSS. There are times that it makes sense for developers to edit style sheets, but they should be rare. For example, in a recent project, we had dozens of modal popups for which initial dimensions were to be specified in a style sheet. I happened to be the long pole in the tent at the time, as the UI was undergoing major modifications for use on a tablet. Without the initial dimensions, the content of the modals couldn't be viewed. Since I had other priorities, it made sense for a developer to run through and enter dimensions in the style sheet. But most of the time, if I see a developer's name listed as the last one to check in a change to a CSS file, I'll do a quick diff to see what they changed. That rarely occurs, because the developers understand the division of responsibilities. Frankly, I hope there are developers who have the same reaction when they see my name on a .js file. I know enough to be dangerous, and while I do test my changes, I'd feel better knowing one of them was checking my work.

The point of declaring CSS ownership isn't to deny others from touching it, but to assign responsibility for quality control, maintenance, and best practices. Too often, CSS isn't treated as *real code*, and as a result, it gets neglected. Your style sheets end up resembling your kitchen junk drawer. Teams are tripping over spaghetti selectors that tie specificity knots in the UI. How often do you add a class to an HTML element expecting to see a certain style applied, but nothing happens, because it's being overridden by some other selector? Have you ever been hesitant to change a style because you're afraid it'll have unintended consequences? Do you ever have trouble tracing a visual attribute on your screen to the style that's applying it? Do you have to perform searches against your entire CSS directory because you don't know which style sheet a particular selector will be in? These are all signs that nobody is taking ownership of the CSS. Somebody has to do it, and it may as well be the people who are going to be working in it the most.

When designers own the CSS, we're responsible for defining how the style sheets will be organized for a given project and the formatting standards that must be followed. More importantly, we must define the architecture of classes that will be utilized, keeping in mind namespaces and inheritance. Do these terms frighten you? Fear not; the following chapters will instruct you on best practices for managing and maintaining your style sheets. For now, I just want to impress upon you the importance of taking ownership of the CSS and the responsibility that it entails.

STYLE SHEET AS DESIGN SPECIFICATION

I spoke quite a bit about the importance of documentation in Chapter 3. You may remember that I try to only document what must be communicated to the developers or the customer. When the person who designed the UI is also the one implementing it, there's a lot of information that can be translated directly from a sketch or mockup to CSS. Take the portion of a UI mockup created in Photoshop in Figure 4.2, for example.

FIGURE 4.2

Data entry keypad

Each key on the keypad has a width and height. There's a certain amount of spacing between the keys. There's a color gradient that gives the keys dimension. There's a font, font size, font color, and font style that defines the numbers, which are centered within the keys. You can't tell in the static image, but there's an intent for the keys to highlight when hovered over and change to show that they're depressed. There's also a disabled state for the keys. I could go on, but you probably get the picture. There's a lot to specify if you want to recreate this exactly in HTML. You could spend a good bit of time drawing arrows and labeling parts with dimensions and color values. You may as well save that time by entering the values directly into a style sheet, which eventually must be done by somebody anyway. Depending on the complexity of a screen, it may even take less time to implement it in HTML and CSS than it would to create a detailed visual design specification. One thing you can be sure of is that it'll take less time than doing both. But, there's an even greater benefit.

When I have to make a change to a Photoshop mockup, it can take some time. I'm not talking about a little change on one screen, mind you—I'm referring to a change that's going to be reflected in many screens, maybe all of them. For example, what if you decide to shrink the height of your global navigation bar by 20 pixels or change your link color. Let's say you have 50 screens. That's going to take a lot of time. And then, you have to open your specification document in InDesign and adjust it to account for the changes in the linked screens. However, to make the same change effective through all of your screens in CSS, all you have to do is change a single value in your style sheet. It takes seconds. If you can get your design into code as soon as possible, you'll save yourself a lot of time when you make revisions.

Part II of this book focuses on web design—partly because the majority of UX professionals are doing web-based work, and partly because it's an ideal situation for designers. We're dealing with languages that we can understand without going back to school for another degree. CSS, in particular, draws from our own visual design language. There are many benefits for designers who implement their designs, but with great power comes great responsibility. We have to learn to treat HTML and CSS as *real code*. There's a discipline to its use, and we should approach it with the same rigor that the developers we work with employ. I hope you don't find that too daunting. It's really not as difficult as it may sound, especially if you have the right tools.

Tooling Up

5

I love tools. I geek out over the right tool for a job. When I was an undergraduate student, I had a tackle box full of pencils, pens, charcoal, erasers, ink, paint, brushes, etc. Once I started in the graphic design program, the contents of the box changed somewhat. I had a compass, triangle, T-square, cork-backed rulers, markers, plaka, scissors, X-acto blades, and the like. I also had Iomega Zip disks. I started learning the plethora of software tools that were available: Freehand, Photoshop, QuarkXpress, Director, Infini-D, Morph, and Authorware. The applications kept changing—Pagemill to GoLive to Dreamweaver. These days, my toolbox still has the Adobe standards, which I use regularly, but they share space with a host of applications that I've been introduced to through my involvement with development. They aren't all design tools, but they're the right tools for the job, and they're every bit as important to my successful delivery of great user experiences.

I alluded to a number of tools in Chapter 3 that you should be using if you expect to integrate with your development team. We're going to take a closer look at some of these, as well as tools specifically for front-end web development. Knowing what tools are available to you, and what you should be using them for, will put you well on your way to being an effective contributor during implementation.

INTEGRATED DEVELOPMENT ENVIRONMENT

If you're working on enterprise web applications, your development team is likely going to be using an integrated development environment (IDE) like Eclipse, Netbeans, or Microsoft Visual Studio. An IDE combines a lot of tools needed for development into one package with a common UI. It'll likely include the source code editor, a debugger, build automation tools, and a host of capabilities for organizing, searching, and viewing the codebase. Many of them support cross-platform development in multiple languages. It makes it relatively easy for a development team to get started on a new project or add new members. Everyone gets the same configuration.

I'm all for using the developers' tools, and you may very well find it beneficial to use your team's IDE, but I think that's overkill. The tooling needed by a designer that will be contributing HTML and CSS is much lighter than the needs of a software engineer. I don't need to be able to compile code to see the changes I make, and I won't be doing any debugging that I can't do directly in a web browser. Of course, that also gives me the flexibility to select my own tools, a luxury the developers don't necessarily have. Perhaps I'm being self-serving, but there does seem to be reasonable justification for making a distinction between the front-end and back-end development environments, as long as they don't step on each other's toes. Many modern web application teams don't use IDEs at all. Your front-end developers should agree on their own development environment—not an IDE, but a set of tools that the team will standardize on.

Your toolbox should contain the following:

• Code editor
• Browsers and their respective development tools
• File comparison tool
• Version control client

CHOOSE YOUR WEAPON

If you're going to be working on code, the first step is to select your editor. Your decision will be based on what exactly you intend to use it for. I primarily work on HTML and CSS with a little JavaScript thrown in. Occasionally, I've found myself editing XML. A lot of you probably have to deal with PHP, and some of you may need to work in Ruby—languages I have little to no experience with. Know, too, that I'm a Mac user of over 20 years, so I'm much more knowledgeable about the tools available on that platform. I'm very particular about my tools, and I believe strongly that the Mac OS is a superior tool for the work I do, so I won't make any apologies about that. I'm going to provide an overview here of several tools that I'm familiar with and recommend. The important thing isn't necessarily to pick one of them, but to understand what is available. You should at least have a grasp of the kind of features you're looking for, and then you can evaluate tools by your own preferences.

There are two types of editors: general text and HTML. General text editors focus on the act of writing code, regardless of the language. They keep the UI simple, but may still have robust capabilities. HTML editors have many more features, such as site management and WYSIWYG editing. They're specifically designed for web development, so they take a few steps down the IDE road, integrating capabilities that web developers will find useful. They are both valuable, and I recommend you select one of each.

General text editors

What I value most in a general text editor is the ability to open and edit any file. It may be an XML, XSLT, or CSS file I've grabbed out of Safari's Web Inspector. I don't care if it's missing an extension, and the OS doesn't know what it is; I need a can opener that will let me see the file's content. I keep TextWrangler in my dock expressly for this purpose. It's a free, stripped-down version of Bare Bones Software's BBEdit. It really is general, and it's useful for more than editing code. It has a powerful, multifile find-and-replace tool and a basic file comparison capability. It's quick to launch, and it'll open anything thrown at it. I wouldn't want to do much coding in it, just as I wouldn't want to use a pocket knife to assemble furniture, but a pocket knife comes in really handy when you need it, as does TextWrangler.

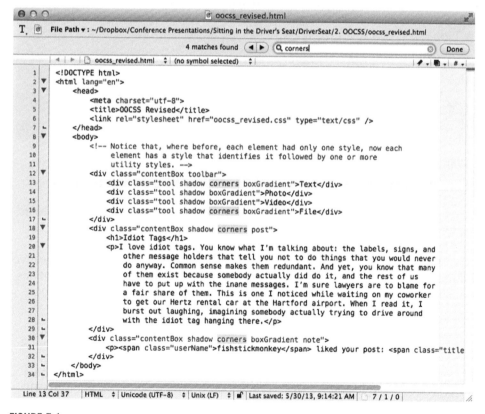

FIGURE 5.1

TextWrangler

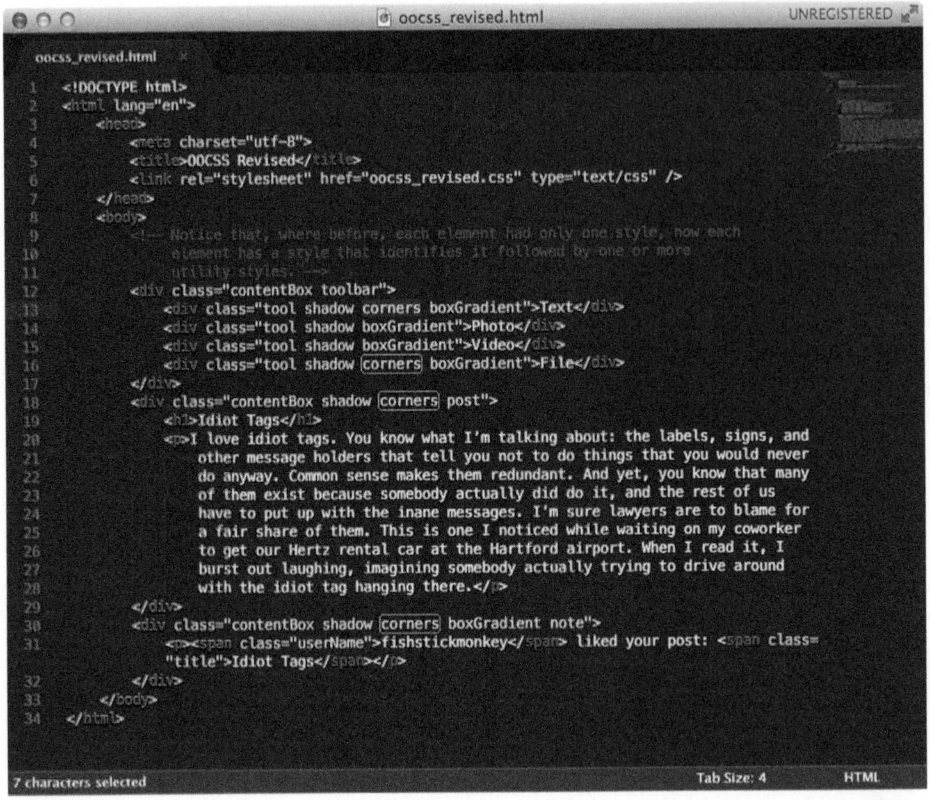

FIGURE 5.2

Sublime Text

Of course, many developers, and even designers, swear by their text editors for web development. I already mentioned BBEdit, which is quite popular on the Mac. TextMate is another that has a solid following. Sublime Text is the newest entry in this category. It's cross-platform and has some rather innovative features. What makes any one of these a good tool? Here is a list of capabilities you should look for in your code editor:

- *Syntax coloring:* The application understands the syntax of the language you're writing and uses color to differentiate among elements, attributes, values, variables, comments, etc. Never code without it.

- *Line numbers:* Listing a line number is the way most errors are reported for debugging purposes, and it makes communication easier among team members.

- *Code folding:* This allows you to collapse sections of your code, based on the hierarchy. I frequently use this to hide long blocks of JavaScript in the pages I work with.

```
1    <!DOCTYPE html>
2    <html lang="en">
3        <head>
4            <meta charset="utf-8">
5            <title>Contact List</title>
6            <link rel="stylesheet" href="contactList_complete.css" type="text/css" />
7
8            <script language="javascript" type="text/javascript">
9                var contactList;
10
11               function init() {
12                   contactList = document.querySelector('.contactList');
13               }
14
15               function toggleLabels() {
16                   contactList.classList.toggle('labelsOn');
17               }
18
19               function togglePhotos() {
20                   contactList.classList.toggle('photosOn');
21               }
22
23               function toggleFavorites() {
24                   contactList.classList.toggle('all');
25               }
26           </script>
27
28       </head>
```

FIGURE 5.3

JavaScript block prior to folding in Espresso

```
1    <!DOCTYPE html>
2    <html lang="en">
3        <head>
4            <meta charset="utf-8">
5            <title>Contact List</title>
6            <link rel="stylesheet" href="contactList_complete.css" type="text/css" />
7
8        ▶    <script language="javascript" type="text/javascript">···</script>
27
28       </head>
```

FIGURE 5.4

JavaScript block after folding

- *Auto-indent:* Also based on the hierarchy, the application can automatically indent lines, keeping your code sensibly structured.

- *Auto-completion:* This one is especially important. I know a lot about HTML and CSS. I understand the syntax. However, I can't always remember everything perfectly. With auto-completion, I can begin typing, and the application will suggest possibilities. For example, let's say you're writing a style for a `<table>`, and you know there are several border declarations that you can control, but you can't remember exactly what they all are. You just know that they start with "border," so you type it and are immediately presented with a list of all of the declarations that start with "border" (e.g. `border-color`, `border-style`, `border-width`, etc.).

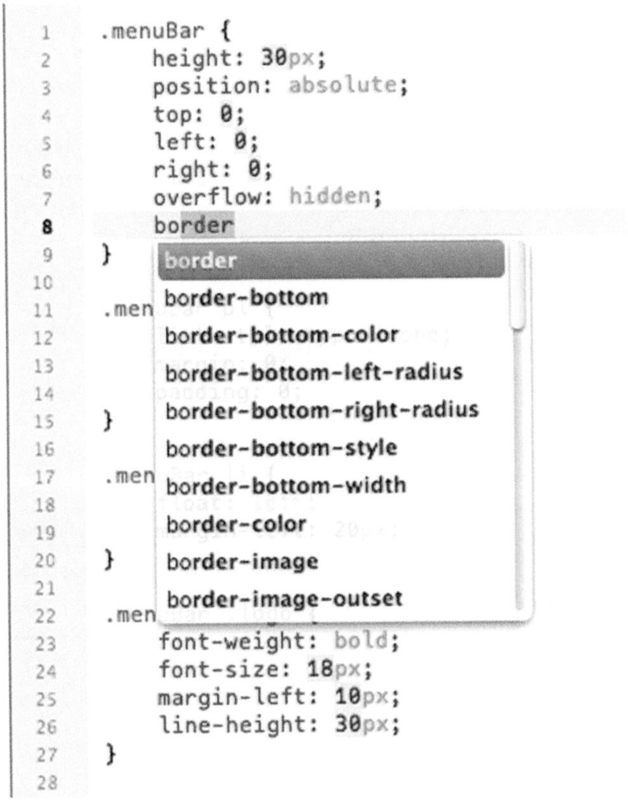

```
1    .menuBar {
2        height: 30px;
3        position: absolute;
4        top: 0;
5        left: 0;
6        right: 0;
7        overflow: hidden;
8        border
9    }
10
11   .men   border
12          border-bottom
13          border-bottom-color
14          border-bottom-left-radius
15   }      border-bottom-right-radius
16          border-bottom-style
17   .men   border-bottom-width
18
19          border-color
20   }      border-image
21
22   .men   border-image-outset
23          font-weight: bold;
24          font-size: 18px;
25          margin-left: 10px;
26          line-height: 30px;
27   }
28
```

FIGURE 5.5

Auto-completion suggestions in Espresso

Now, some tools take this farther than others. A really good tool will not just enter a single opening tag, but will enter an entire element, complete with attributes that it'll allow you to tab between to enter values. For example, if you type "d" and then press Enter with "div" selected, you might get this: `<div id=""></div>`. Notice that the id attribute is selected. You have the choice of typing over it, say with a class attribute, or tabbing into it to enter the ID. Once you get the hang of it, this really speeds up coding. It's worth noting that good code completion for JavaScript is generally only supported in the more sophisticated editors and IDEs due to the dynamic nature of the language.

- *Auto-pairing:* This is another significant timesaver. The editor knows that every opening tag must be closed, so when you type `</`, it checks to see

what the most recent, unclosed element is and finishes the tag for you: `</div>`. Some editors will highlight the paired tags when one is selected or provide other shortcuts based on the pairing.

- *Snippets:* Many editors have the ability to hold blocks of regularly used code for quick insertion.

- *Find and replace:* Powerful search capabilities are a must, and the more robust, the better. Sublime Text has a rather spectacular multiselection capability that allows you to find and select multiple occurrences of the current word. Start typing, and they all get replaced at once. I also highly recommend that you pick a tool that can perform searches across multiple files.

- *Multiple views:* This is a matter of preference, but I find tabbed windows to be very helpful when dealing with a lot of files. Some editors provide views for having two documents up side-by-side or even two views of the same document—a blessing if you have to jump back and forth between two sections of your file.

There are many, many more features that a code editor could have, but this list gives the basic capabilities you should look for. Most applications these days have a free trial, so you can take them for a test drive and see how they measure up. If you're already using a text editor and would like to trick it out a bit, take a look at Emmet. It supports most of the editors mentioned and will give you a powerful cadre of shortcuts, snippets, and automated actions.

As I said, you should have a general text editor in your pocket for pure utility. Many people prefer them over HTML editors, and some can even be extended to include additional capabilities like FTP. When it comes to serious front-end web development, however, I prefer something a little beefier.

Table 5.1 General Text Editors

Tool	Developer	Platform	URL
TextWrangler	Bare Bones Software	Mac	*www.barebones.com*
BBEdit	Bare Bones Software	Mac	*www.barebones.com*
TextMate	MacroMates	Mac	*www.macromates.com*
Sublime Text	Sublime HQ	Mac, Windows, Linux	*www.sublimetext.com*
Emmet	Sergey Chikuyonok		*www.emmet.io*

HTML editors

A powerful HTML editor offers everything found in a general text editor, but adds more features specific to web development. There are two such tools that I encourage you to look into: MacRabbit's Espresso and Panic's Coda. These are both Mac-only offerings. I've been told by workshop attendees that TopStyle is a worthy equivalent for Windows. So, what do these HTML editors give you that makes them so much more useful than a general text editor? Prepare to salivate.

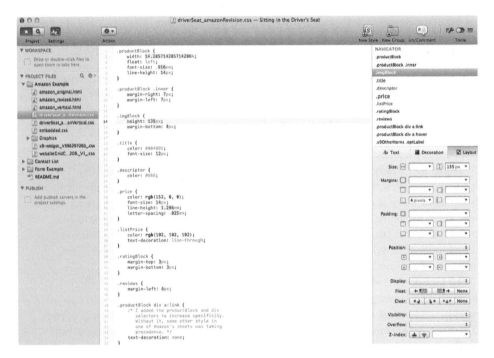

FIGURE 5.6

Espresso

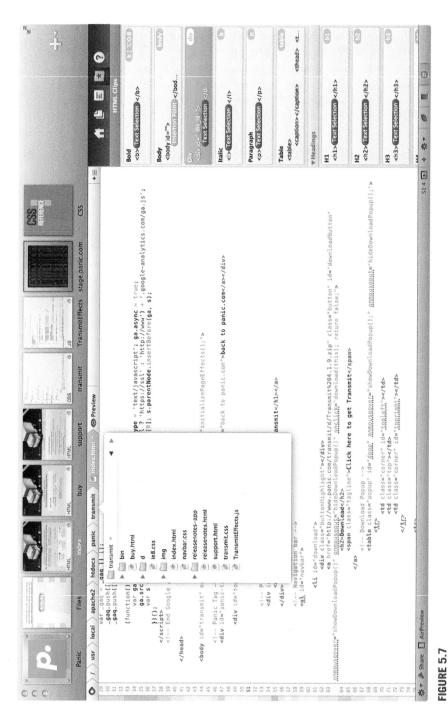

FIGURE 5.7

Coda

- *Projects/sites:* These tools understand that you aren't likely working on a single web page. You have an entire site or web application with HTML files, CSS files, graphic files, and any number of other file types, libraries, and media objects. The directory structure they're in is important also. A good editor will allow you to quickly switch between files, rearrange your files, add and delete them, and search across the entire project. Many of them go as far as to provide management of multiple projects.

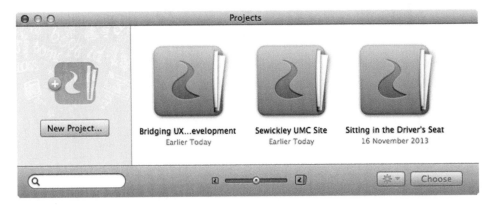

FIGURE 5.8

Espresso's projects window

- *FTP:* Built-in FTP capabilities allow you to synchronize your local files with those on your server. The application checks to see which files have changed, been added, or been deleted, and allows you to control what happens during the sync. Espresso even has a setting that will automatically upload a file every time you save it. Certainly this is useful when maintaining a website, but I employ it for application development also. More on that later.

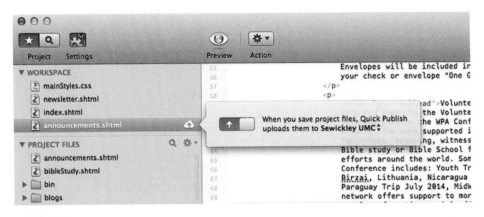

FIGURE 5.9

Espresso's FTP on save feature

- *CSS editor:* Both Espresso and Coda have GUIs for editing CSS that integrate beautifully with the text editor. You can enter values into fields and watch the declarations be added to your styles. You say you don't remember the order the values should be listed for specifying padding? Enter the values into individual fields for top, right, bottom, and left, and they'll be written in the correct order. But this isn't just a handicap for people who can't write CSS from scratch. I fluidly move back and forth between the GUI and the code. Sometimes, it's faster to press the Bold button than to type out `font-weight: bold;`.

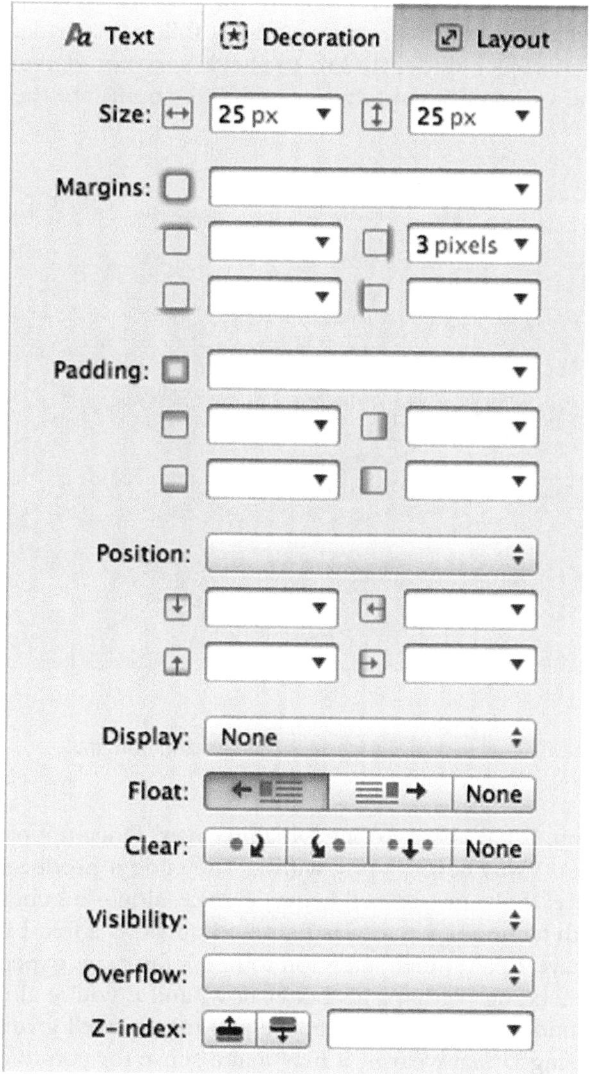

FIGURE 5.10

Espresso's CSS editor

- *Live preview:* This is the pièce de résistance. While you're typing (or using the CSS GUI) the preview of your page updates in real time. You don't have to save your file and then press Refresh in a browser window every time you want to see the change you made. This, more than anything, changes the way you work with HTML and CSS. Coding is no longer just an implementation activity. It's truly a design activity in which you can experiment with immediate feedback.

- *Inspector:* The preview isn't just a preview. Hover over an element to see its boundaries. Select an element to see which classes are successfully targeting it and then trace them back to the files in which they reside. Once an element is selected, you can easily follow a breadcrumb trail up the document object model (DOM) to check ancestor elements. I can't overstate the value of having these capabilities built into the editor.

FIGURE 5.11

Espresso's live preview, demonstrating its inspector and breadcrumb trail

Yes, I hear you. What about Adobe Dreamweaver? Once upon a time, I did use Dreamweaver. I was never happy with it. The code it produced made my developers cranky. It always seemed heavy, clunky, slow—a behemoth struggling to keep pace with technology that was light and quick as a fox. I haven't used it in years, nor have I paid much attention to it. It's far more expensive than the tools I'm recommending. Perhaps it's better now, and if you're already paying for a Creative Cloud subscription, I suppose you may as well give it a try. If you're already using Dreamweaver, it may make sense for you to continue doing so, maximizing your investment in the Adobe ecosystem. You're welcome to it. I'm happy with "an elegant weapon for a more civilized age."

To their credit, Adobe introduced an experimental editor named Brackets, which has been open-sourced. It has some really interesting features, such as inline CSS editing. This allows you to put your cursor on an element in your HTML, press Command/Control + E, and see the styles targeting the element directly in the same page. This could save a lot of time, especially on projects of the size I often work on. It also integrates with your browser (Chrome only, so far) to provide a live view. This tool is still early in its development, but it's already quite useful and shows a lot of promise.

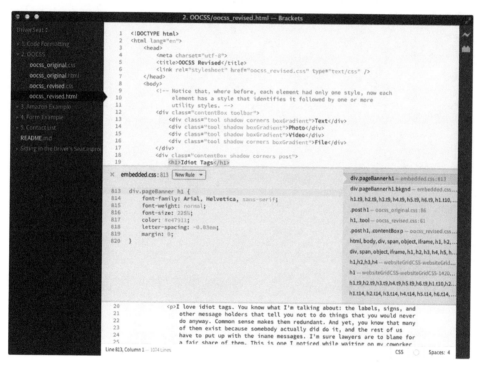

FIGURE 5.12

Brackets

The future of HTML editors

I'm writing this paragraph in November 2013. We work in a rapidly changing field, and our tools adapt, hopefully at a similar pace. Even now, the next generation of editors is on the horizon. I have my eye on Macaw, "the code-savvy web design tool." It looks to be everything we designers have been dreaming about for years—the promise that Adobe just hasn't been able to deliver. It has flexible, WYSIWYG layout tools that mimic creating a mockup as we would in Photoshop, but at the same time, it's producing model object-oriented CSS (OOCSS) as I'll be teaching you in Chapter 7. Does this mean we're almost to the point at which this book becomes useless? Can designers have the same amount of control, participating in implementation, without knowing how to code? There are those who believe that. I'm not holding my breath, but it's becoming easier.

FIGURE 5.13

Macaw

Table 5.2 HTML Editors			
Tool	**Developer**	**Platform**	**URL**
Espresso	MacRabbit	Mac	*www.macrabbit.com*
Coda	Panic	Mac	*www.panic.com*
TopStyle	TopStyle	Windows	*www.topstyle4.com*
Dreamweaver	Adobe	Mac, Windows	*www.adobe.com*
Brackets	Adobe/Open Source	Mac, Windows, Linux	*www.brackets.io*
Macaw	Macaw	Mac	*www.macaw.co*

BROWSER DEVELOPER TOOLS

As of this writing, there are four major desktop browsers: Safari, Chrome, Firefox, and Internet Explorer (IE). Each one has its own development tools that allow us to examine and manipulate the code. Safari and Chrome both run on WebKit, the open-source engine developed by Apple, as do the majority of mobile browsers. So, there are really three engines we have to implement to. As I mentioned, the HTML editors have excellent preview capabilities, but they rely on the WebKit engine to render pages. That's enough to get about 95% of the way there. If your page displays properly in your preview, then you can reasonably expect it to display the same way in all modern browsers. However, we can't just assume; we have to test our work in multiple browsers and even multiple versions, especially where IE is concerned. Sometimes, there are differences in the way each browser interprets the standards. IE, in particular, has had a long and bumpy road toward compliance. When we run into these discrepancies, we have to figure out how to work around them, and that means troubleshooting directly in the browser. Of course, we aren't always building pages from scratch. Probably more often than not, there's already a site or application in existence. The browser developer tools are just the thing for trying out minor modifications or troubleshooting bugs. Let's take a look.

Safari Web Inspector

To access Safari's Web Inspector, you must first enable the Develop menu by selecting the "Show Develop menu in menu bar" option on the Advanced tab of Safari's Preferences pane.

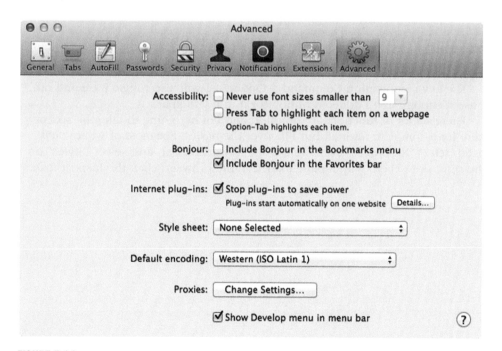

FIGURE 5.14

Safari's Preferences pane

Now, in the Develop menu, you can select "Show Web Inspector."

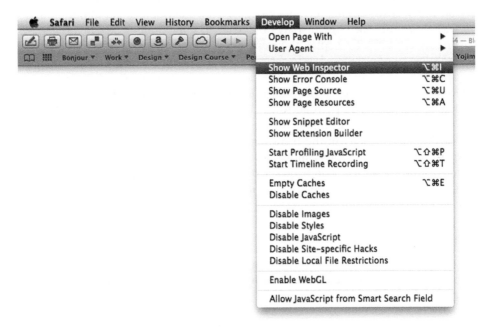

FIGURE 5.15

Develop menu

The key combination Command + Option + I will also toggle it on and off. I use it enough that I added a button for it in my toolbar.

There's a lot of functionality on offer, and I'm not going to take the space here for a complete tutorial, but I'll cover the basics. For most of what you'll need, select "Resources" at the left of the navigation bar, and select "Styles" on the right side. Then, with a page loaded in the browser, click the Inspect icon.

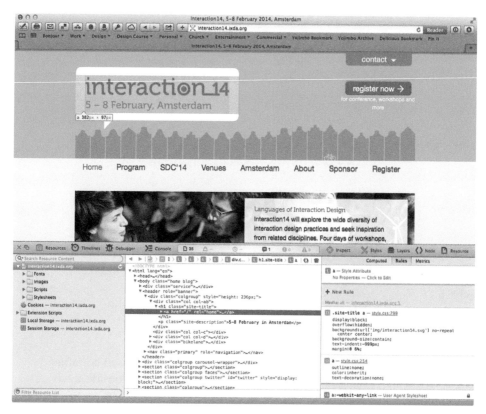

FIGURE 5.16

Safari Web Inspector

   In this mode, you can move your cursor over the page and see elements highlight. Any padding or margins will be depicted, as well as the boundaries of the element. Clicking an element on the page will highlight it in the DOM tree below. Consequently, clicking a DOM node in the tree will highlight the element on the page. Any styles targeting the selected element will be listed on the right. It'll tell you which style sheet the style resides in and the line number where you can find it. Styles are listed in precedence order, with the most specific at the top and least specific at the bottom. It'll tell you what styles are being inherited from other elements, and it'll line out styles that are being overridden by more specific selectors.

FIGURE 5.17

Overridden, inherited styles

That in itself is quite helpful, but the real kicker is that it's all editable! Hover over a style, and you'll be presented with checkboxes beside every declaration. Uncheck one, and that declaration is turned off. The page immediately updates. Click a value, and you can edit it. Click a declaration, and you can change it to a different one (e.g., padding to margin). Insert your cursor at the end of a line and press Enter. Now you can add a new declaration. Click New Rule to add a completely new rule, selector, declarations, and all. Notice, also, the checkboxes at the top of the CSS list: Active, Focus, Hover, and Visited. If you want to see and edit a style that gets applied on Hover, for example, check its box. That will apply the hover state to the object, and you'll now see any styles targeting the element with the :hover pseudo-selector in the list.

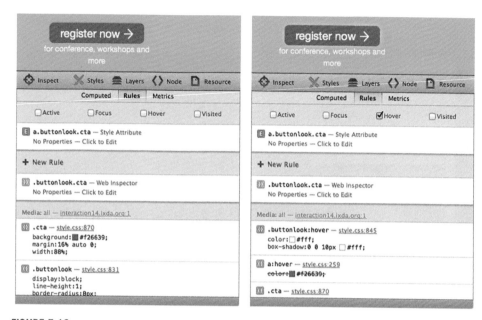

FIGURE 5.18

Selecting the Hover state

It isn't just the CSS that can be edited, either. Double-click a DOM node to make changes to the HTML. Assign classes, change a `<span>` to be a `<div>`. The sky is the limit. With this kind of power, you'll be able to not only troubleshoot a problem and identify its cause, but try out potential solutions and know exactly what changes need to be made in the source code. I've been known to completely revise a screen directly in the browser and then copy the code out of the Web Inspector to paste into the original file.

Chrome

As I explained earlier, Chrome is built on top of WebKit, and as it happens, the Web Inspector is part of the WebKit engine. Google has laid things out differently, but all the same functionality is there. To open it in Chrome, open the View menu, at the bottom of which you'll find the Developer menu. The Developer Tools option is what you're looking for. If you learn how to use one of them, reorienting yourself to the other won't be too difficult.

FIGURE 5.19

Chrome

Firebug

Before the Web Inspector was introduced in Safari, there was Firebug, an extension for Firefox. Firebug really defined what developer tools in a browser should be, and while WebKit has surpassed it in some ways (e.g., the checkboxes for pseudo-states), there's a lot to love in Firebug. Again, it's laid out similarly and has the same basic capabilities. Because it's an open-source extension, you'll have to download and install it separately. This can be a little bothersome when Firefox is updated and breaks Firebug, but it's developed by Mozilla, so they're pretty good about keeping it up-to-date. A benefit of this arrangement, however, is that Firebug itself is extensible. There are all manner of extensions for Firebug. For example, cssUpdater will sync changes you make in Firebug back to your original CSS files.

FIGURE 5.20

Firebug

Firefox

Recently, Firefox has been coming on strong with their own, built-in developer tools. They work similarly to those already described, but there are a couple of innovative features worth making special note of.

FIGURE 5.21

Firefox developer tools

They have added a 3D view that allows you to tilt the webpage on a center axis. Each element is given a bit of thickness and presented as if it is stacked on top of its parenting element. I've only played with it briefly, so it remains to be seen whether or not I'll find it to be a useful tool, but it is an interesting way of viewing a page.

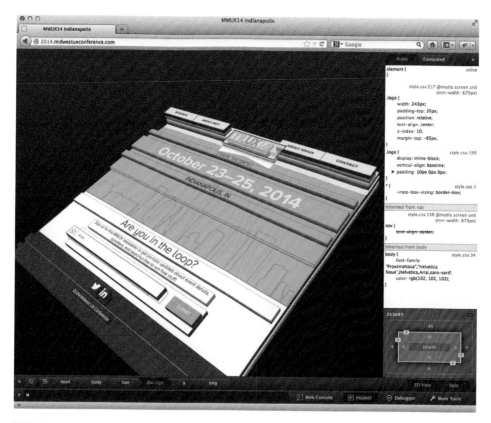

FIGURE 5.22

Firefox's 3D view

Firefox also sports a responsive design view, which allows you to resize the contents of the webpage without resizing the browser window. A menu provides standard screen sizes, and a "rotate" button swaps the dimensions between portrait and landscape.

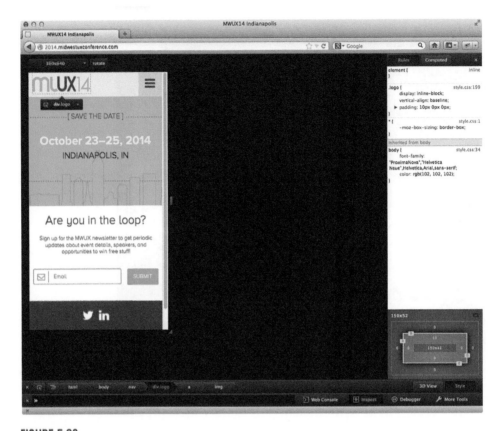

FIGURE 5.23

Firefox's responsive design view

IE F12

And then there's IE. As in most things, IE has been behind the other browsers in the improvement of its developer tools. As the name suggests, you can press F12 to open it. The layout is, once again, very similar, as are the capabilities. IE is just a little less intuitive and kind of clunky. That's to be expected. However, be happy that the tools are there, because IE is where you're most likely to find those discrepancies that you'll have to fix. It'll be much easier to troubleshoot them in the F12 tools than to play a frustrating game of trial and error, making a change in your source code, saving, and refreshing IE over and over again.

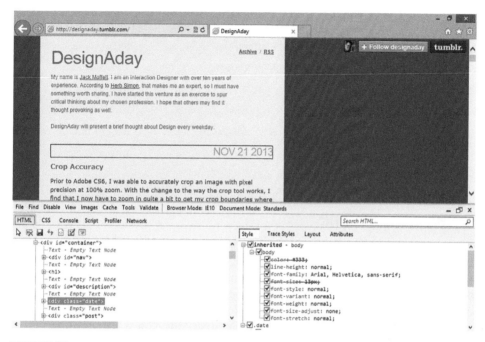

FIGURE 5.24

IE F12

There's one key feature in IE's tools that I want to make special note of, and that's the Browser Mode menu. There have been significant changes to the way IE renders HTML and CSS from version to version, which can give you a migraine as you test your implementation. This menu will make your life a little bit easier. Instead of requiring separate installations of the various versions of IE, you can simply select the version you want to test in the menu. IE will render the page as that version will.

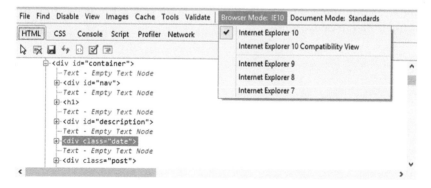

FIGURE 5.25

Browser mode

Table 5.3 Browser Development Tools

Tool	Developer	Platform	URL
Safari	Apple	Mac, Windows	*www.apple.com*
Chrome	Google	Mac, Windows, Linux	*www.google.com*
Firefox	Mozilla	Mac, Windows, Linux	*www.mozilla.org/firefox*
Firebug	Mozilla	Mac, Windows, Linux	*www.getfirebug.com*
Internet Explorer	Microsoft	Windows	*www.microsoft.com*

DIFFING AND MERGING

Working in a team means sharing files. When you share hundreds of files during a project that runs for months, there's a pretty good chance that occasionally two people will end up making changes to the same chunk of code. In fact, it's more likely to happen to you than one of the developers. The developers tend to have their tasking organized such that they don't have to work on many of the same files. Meanwhile, every file you work on, other than the style sheets, will also require a developer's attention. So, you both may end up working on the same file over a period of time, and when you check in, you may find that there's a merge conflict and you have to decide what code to keep. You could try to eyeball it, but why do that when there are tools that can help? (Insert your own Tim "The Tool Man" Taylor grunt here.)

The process of comparing two files to find differences is called *running a diff* or *diffing*. I already mentioned a free tool that does a decent job. TextWrangler will open two files side-by-side with a third window below listing all of the differences found between them. Select a difference from the list and see the difference highlighted in both files. Buttons allow you to then pick the version you want to keep, copying it to one file or the other. This process of selecting and combining pieces into a new version of the file is referred to as *performing a merge* or *merging*.

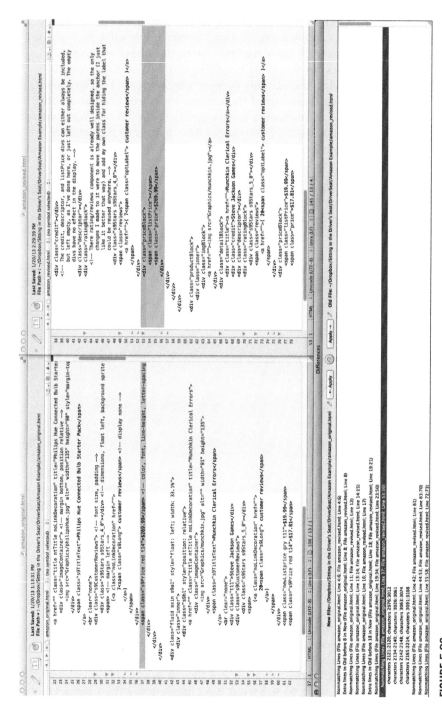

FIGURE 5.26

TextWrangler diff

Another one that's freely available on the Mac, FileMerge, installs with Xcode. It's not the easiest application to get to, as it's packaged within Xcode, but it'll run as a standalone application. You just have to right-click Xcode and select "Show Package Contents." FileMerge will be in the Applications folder. Once you launch it, it'll prompt you to select a file to show on the left and another to show on the right. This display is more elegant than TextWrangler's. It's a single window that highlights all of the changes at once. Use the arrow keys to move up and down from change to change. Use the left and right arrow keys to select the version that you want to keep. The arrows in the middle column will point to the version that will be kept. Then you can save the merge as a new file.

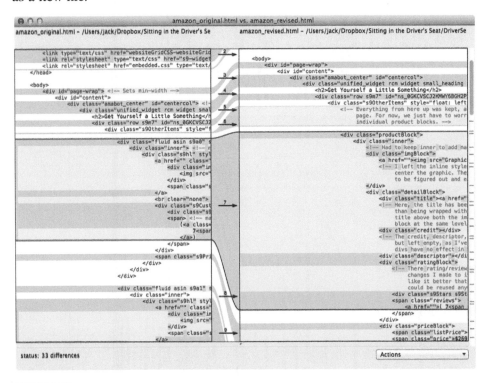

FIGURE 5.27

FileMerge

TextWrangler or FileMerge will get the job done, but the application I recommend, especially for designers, is Kaleidoscope from Black Pixel. This is the ultimate tool for file comparisons. Like FileMerge, it has a one-window view that highlights all changes at once, but it provides three different ways to view them, and it'll allow you to compare three files at once. This capability comes in handy when you want to see what has changed in a file over several versions. In addition to comparing text files, Kaleidoscope will compare two different directories, allowing you to copy files between them. And if that's not enough to get your attention, it'll also diff image files. That's just nuts.

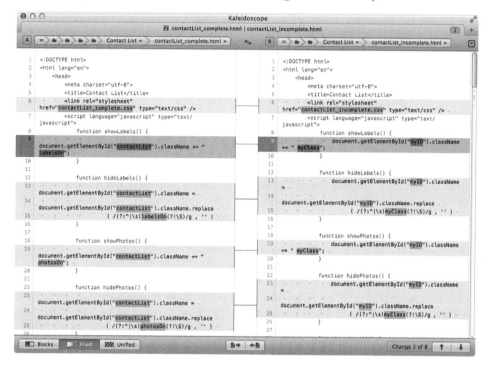

FIGURE 5.28

Kaleidoscope

Table 5.4 File Comparison

Tool	Developer	Platform	URL
TextWrangler	Bare Bones Software	Mac	www.barebones.com
FileMerge	Apple	Mac	www.developer.apple.com
Kaleidoscope	Black Pixel	Mac	www.blackpixel.com

VERSION CONTROL

I was surprised to find that 15% of the survey respondents claimed that nobody at their company uses version control software. I tried to find some kind of trend that would explain this, but there wasn't one. Regardless of company size, team size, company type, or type of work, that 15% was evenly distributed. To think that there are that many development teams out there tight-rope walking without a safety net boggles my mind.

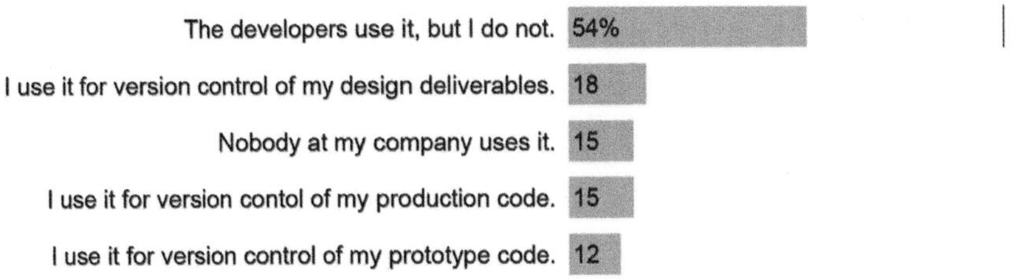

The developers use it, but I do not.	54%
I use it for version control of my design deliverables.	18
Nobody at my company uses it.	15
I use it for version contol of my production code.	15
I use it for version control of my prototype code.	12

FIGURE 5.29

Do you use version control software?

But perhaps I'm getting ahead of myself. Many of you may not even know of what I speak. A version control system (VCS) (also referred to as revision control or source control) is what is used to manage the changes to your code base by multiple people over time. It keeps track of every version of each file in its repository. When you check out a file, you get a local copy of it that you can work with, thus referred to as a *working copy*. When you're done working on it, you check it back in (or *commit* it). At that point, a new version of the file is copied into the repository while the previous version is maintained. While it's possible to lock a file and keep others from checking it out, the beauty of the system is that multiple people can check out the same file and work on it at the same time. Each time a person checks the file back in, it's merged with any other versions that have been checked in since the time the file was checked out, so the most recent version of the file will include everyone's changes. If you've edited part of the file that changed since you checked it out, the VCS will notify you of a merge conflict, indicating what parts of the file are in question. You must then decide what to do with those portions of the file before checking in.

Because the repository contains every version of every file, you can, at any point, retrieve any version of any file. Of course, you usually check in multiple files at once, so the entire repository is versioned for each check-in. If you need to, you can roll back to a previous revision, making it the current version (referred to as the *head* or *tip*). A VCS protects your team from losing anything. It protects your team from really messing things up. You can always go back to a previous state in which everything was hunky-dory. In addition, a nonlocking VCS allows your team to work in parallel without fear of clobbering each other, because it can automatically merge most changes made to the same file. You only have to manually merge (using your file comparison tool) when two developers have edited the same lines of code.

Beyond the basics, a VCS manages versions of your entire codebase, referred to as *branches*. For example, let's say your company has a software product that you sell directly to businesses. Some of your customers are happy to use your product as is, commonly referred to as commercial off-the-shelf (COTS). However, sometimes you get a customer with specialized needs willing to pay for customizations. These are changes that you don't necessarily want to make to the product you sell to everyone, but 90% of your code base is going to be the same, and your new customer will want to continue receiving updates and bug fixes that you make to the core product. In your VCS, you can branch the code. In some VCSs, this will create a separate directory within the repository that you can check out and check in apart from the trunk—the main code base. Other VCSs will only allow you to work on a single branch at a time. The VCS only makes copies of the files that changes are made to, so it doesn't dramatically affect your storage space. At any point, you can merge changes made to the trunk into the branch, updating the customized version of the application. If at any point in time you decide that you want to incorporate some of the changes made in the branch back into the trunk, you can merge in that direction as well. Merge conflicts are likely to arise and will have to be worked out, just as when two developers work on a file in parallel.

The VCS will also keep track of releases through what are termed *tags* (also called *baselines* or *labels*). When you have a version of the code base that you consider to be important, such as a version that was delivered to a customer, you can tag that version. The VCS basically creates a bookmark, making note of the version of every file at that point in time. Then, when you have to refer back to a particular release version, say for a customer support issue, you just check out the tag and the VCS gathers the correct files for you.

I hope you now understand how powerful and critically useful version control is to a team. If you're in that 15% working for companies that don't employ a VCS, you have an opportunity to make a significant contribution to your team simply by suggesting that they start using one. It'll take some work to select one and integrate it into your development process, but there really isn't a question. This is something that you should be doing.

While version control is especially intended for source code, it isn't limited to it. A VCS can store and track any kind of file. You won't have the ability to merge documents, of course, but all of the other capabilities will be just as useful for versioning your sketches, mockups, prototypes, specifications, and any other design artifacts you employ. I religiously check in all of my work files. On one particular project, I have to maintain training materials for three different deployed versions of an application on two platforms in parallel. The trunk is always the most recent version of the application, and there are branches for the two old versions, each with two sets of training materials, one for each platform. I still have to edit each version of the material separately, but at least they're all organized and tracked. It sure beats the heck out of trying to maintain it all in the file system.

I'm most familiar with Subversion (SVN), an open-source VCS developed by the Apache Software Foundation, because that's what my company uses. Subversion integrates with JIRA, our issue tracking system, such that if we enter an issue number into a check-in comment, information about the commit will automatically be written into the JIRA issue with a link into FishEye, another Atlassian product for searching, tracking, and visualizing code changes. We use FishEye for managing code reviews, and while I'm not going to go into a detailed explanation of this, the point is that there are many things to consider when selecting a VCS. Integration with the rest of your development environment is a significant one.

Subversion uses a centralized, client-server model, which means that you must have access to the server on which the repository resides, and you need a piece of software running on your own machine, a client, that will communicate with the server. If your developers are running Windows, they're likely using Tortoise, an SVN client that integrates directly into the Windows file system. Right-click on a folder under version control and you'll have options in your contextual menu to update it, commit it, or do anything else you can possibly do. It works well, it's convenient, and it's free. If you're on Windows, you don't really have any reason to use anything else.

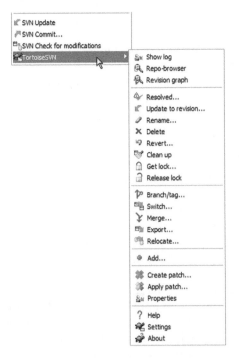

FIGURE 5.30

Tortoise

If you're on a Mac, there aren't any free options—none worth using. Don't get upset, though. As is typical, the Mac clients are outstanding. Personally,

I use Versions from Black Pixel (yes, the same folks that gave us Kaleidoscope), which was the first good client to be released for Mac OSX, but Cornerstone, by Zennaware, looks like it has surpassed Versions in capabilities. Cornerstone recognizes the value in versioning more than just code and provides features for viewing and comparing image files. It has code comparison, merge capabilities, and file editing baked in, and it provides a host of features for avoiding conflicts and merging branches. Both tools integrate with external file comparison tools, including Kaleidoscope and FileMerge, allowing you to select file versions to compare within the SVN client and then send them to the other application.

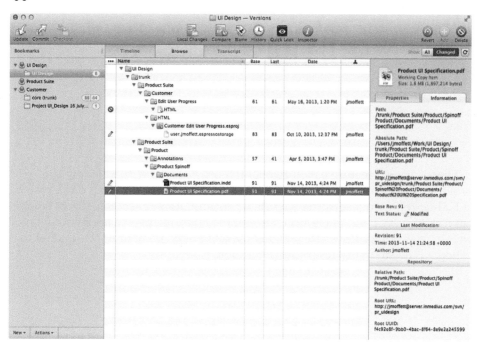

FIGURE 5.31

Versions

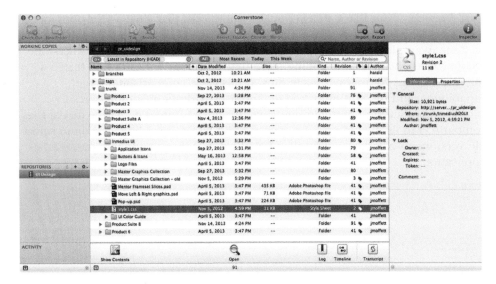

FIGURE 5.32

Cornerstone

There's even a feature called Blame. It'll provide you with a line-by-line listing of who last changed the code in any file version. More than once, I've had a bug reported against the CSS or HTML and, upon checking, discovered that it wasn't my fault. One of the developers made changes without knowing what he was doing. I promise, I didn't make a big deal about it, but I admit to feeling a little smug the rest of the afternoon.

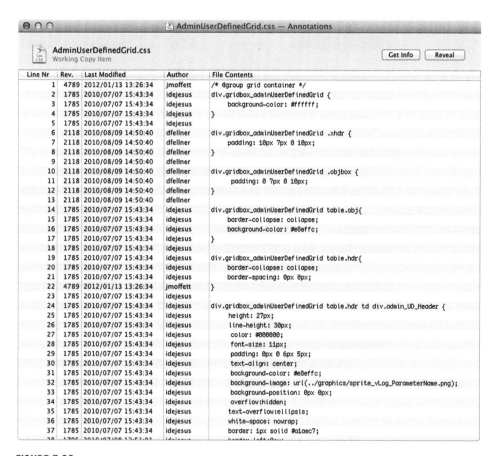

FIGURE 5.33

Blame in versions

A word of caution when working with local files under version control: Be aware that your client is tracking these files by adding invisible files to each folder you have under version control. If you move files around or rename them in the Finder, you can mess things up. Always try to move, copy, and rename version-controlled files through the client.

With the rise of the Internet, a number of open-source VCSs employing a distributed, peer-to-peer model have been introduced, including Git and Mercurial. These allow version control without that central server in what is basically just a bunch of synched working copies. There are clients for these as well, such as Tower and Gitbox on the Mac. SourceTree is available for both Mac and Windows, and it acts as a client for Git and Mercurial.

FIGURE 5.34

Tower

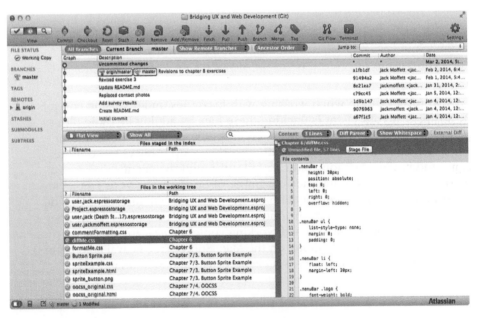

FIGURE 5.35

SourceTree

Git has become enormously popular and is heavily used for open-source development. To facilitate this, however, you still need a repository by which to distribute projects and facilitate communication. GitHub arose to fill that need, offering both the repository and clients for multiple platforms. GitHub is free for public repositories, and that's what we're going to use for the exercises that make up the rest of this book. In fact, it's time for the first exercise now. Please hold onto the bar.

Table 5.5 Version Control

Tool	Developer	Platform	URL
Subversion	Apache	Mac, Windows, Unix, BeOS, OS/2	*www.subversion.apache.org*
TortoiseSVN	Open Source	Windows	*www.tortoisesvn.net*
Versions	Black Pixel	Mac	*www.blackpixel.com*
Cornerstone	Zennaware	Mac	*www.zennaware.com*
Git	Open Source	Mac, Windows, Linux, Solaris	*www.git-scm.com*
GitHub	GitHub	Mac, Windows, Linux	*www.github.com*
Mercurial	Open Source	Mac, Windows, Linux, Solaris	*www.mercurial.selenic.com*
Tower	Fournova	Mac	*www.git-tower.com*
Gitbox	Oleg Andreev	Mac	*www.gitboxapp.com*
SourceTree	Atlassian	Mac, Windows	*www.sourcetreeapp.com*

EXERCISE 1: GIT 'ER DONE!

In this exercise, you'll download the GitHub client and fork the Bridging-UX-and-Web-Development repository.

Note: If you don't want to bother with learning to use a VCS, but you'd still like to get all of the sample code, you can still download the project from GitHub. Instead of signing up for an account, simply click "Explore" and search for Bridging-UX-and-Web-Development. Then press the Download ZIP button.

1. Open your web browser of choice and navigate to *github.com*.

2. Sign up for an account.

3. Once you have an account and are signed in, you'll want to download their native client. Clients are available for Mac, Windows, and Linux.

Assuming their site structure hasn't changed, you can find them here: *https://help.github.com/articles/set-up-git.*

4. Follow their instructions to set up the client. It involves entering a few terminal commands, but don't let that scare you. They're simple, and GitHub's instructions tell you exactly what to do.

5. Back in your browser, click the "Return to GitHub" link. Then, in the search field, type "Bridging-UX-and-Web-Development"—it should come up as a result with my name, "jackmoffett," in front of it. Click on that.

FIGURE 5.36

Bridging-UX-and-Web-Development repository on GitHub

6. Now you're viewing my repository. Welcome! What you're looking for here is the Fork button in the top-right corner of the window. This is going to make you a copy of my repository. You'll be able to edit the files as you please and check them in without affecting my repository at all. Go ahead and press the Fork button.

7. Now you're looking at your own copy of the repository. See? It has your name in front of it. If you haven't already, launch your GitHub client. You'll have to sign in with your GitHub credentials.

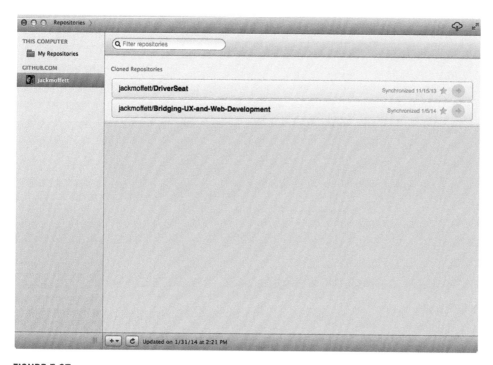

FIGURE 5.37

GitHub client

8. In the left column, you'll see two sections: This Computer, under which will be "My Repositories," and GitHub.com, under which will be your name. Select yourself.

9. Now you'll see the list of your repositories on GitHub. Unless you've been holding out on me, the only one listed is your copy of Bridging-UX-and-Web-Development. Now press the Clone to Computer button. It'll prompt you to save the repository to your local drive. This will be your working copy.

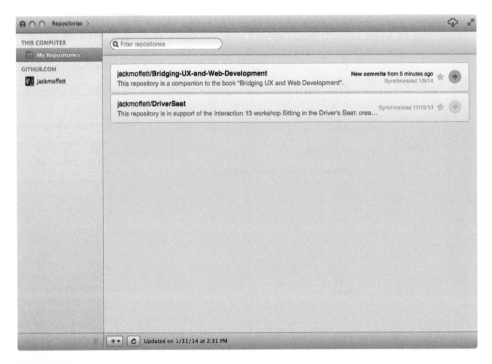

FIGURE 5.38

My Repositories

10. Now select "My Repositories" in the sidebar. Your working copy is listed there. Click the arrow to open it. Now the sidebar allows you to see your history, changes, branches, and settings.

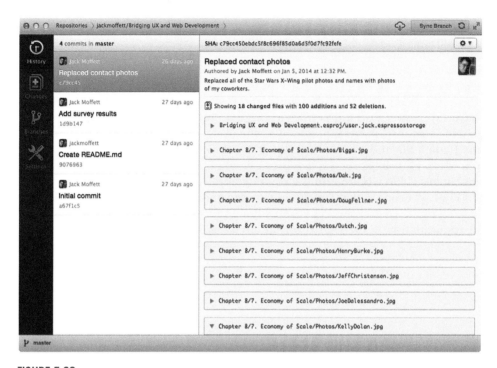

FIGURE 5.39

Bridging-UX-and-Web-Development working copy

That's it! You've completed the first exercise, and now you have all of the files necessary to complete the rest of the exercises in the coming chapters. "You've taken your first step into a much larger world."

PUTTING IT ALL TOGETHER

I've introduced you to a lot of tools, and if it's all new to you, you'll have your work cut out for you trying to adjust your process to incorporate it all. It might help for me to explain my development environment. Understand, however, that I'm working in a software development firm that creates enterprise applications. You may not require as complex a setup.

As you already know, I'm working on a Mac. I'm doing so in a team of developers who are all working on Windows. That can get a little tricky, but when you're doing web development, the platform you use really shouldn't matter. The hardest part is testing in IE, and you can do that either by running a VM directly on your Mac or by accessing a VM on your network. A lot of the work that I do, while web based, requires client software to be installed for disconnected use, and the client only runs on Windows, per the customer's requirements. So, just like every developer on the team, I have a Windows VM set up on the network with the client installed. I can check out the latest code directly from Subversion using Tortoise and rebuild the client when necessary. I also have the FTP service enabled on the VM. I check the project out of Subversion to my Mac using Versions, and that's where I do all of my work. I have Espresso set up to FTP files to the VM. Every time I update my working copy in Versions, I have Espresso sync the updated files to the VM. Every time I edit a file and save it, Espresso FTP's it to the VM. So, the VM is always up-to-date. I'll use Espresso's live preview when I'm building new screens from scratch, but if I'm working on the running application, I'll have to actually run it in Firefox. I can do that locally on my Mac and be 99% sure everything is working right. Then, using Microsoft's Remote Desktop (RDC) for Mac, I'll run the application in IE on the VM for the final test.

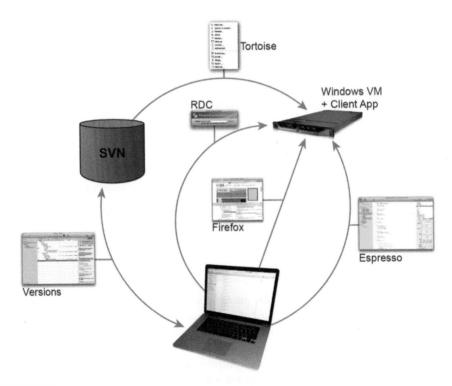

FIGURE 5.40

Example development environment

If you're working on consumer-oriented websites or working for a UX firm, rather than a software development shop, your environment will probably look a lot different. You may be using Git, so you'll need a different client. You may not need to FTP to a VM, but maybe there's a test server you can FTP to. Whatever the case, take things one step at a time. Ask Shelley (You remember Shelley... from Chapter 2) to help you get set up. She won't like it when your mouse scrolls in reverse, but she knows her way around Subversion, and she'll probably be able to point you to some wiki pages about how the developer environments are set up. If you explain to her what you're trying to do, she'll help you figure it out.

Now that you have some tools, let me show you what to do with them.

Formatting Standards

6

I guess I don't need to convince you of the importance of designing things well. But let me impress upon you the need to apply the same meticulous care and attention to detail in your code that you do in anything you'd design. In my experience, designers tend to be rather haphazard with their code. Perhaps that's only because they know it isn't production code. Regardless of the reason, it's a habit we need to break. If you're working on production code, you should be designing it to be usable by yourself and your team. It all starts with formatting standards.

What's one of the first rules of user-centered design—something like, "you're not the user"? Just so, you shouldn't write code for yourself alone. Yes, you're a user of your own code, but you aren't the only one who will be using it during your current development effort, and there will likely be other people who have to maintain it in the future. You should be considerate of your current team and those who will inherit your work. The goal is for the entire code base to look like a single person wrote it. That will make it easier for people new to the project to come up to speed, and it'll make it easier for anyone to maintain.

It's likely that your developers already have formatting standards in place for Java and JavaScript. Their tools provide code style checking and auto-formatting functions that ensure the entire team is following the standards. These tools may apply some basic formatting to HTML, but they're likely set to their defaults unless your team includes front-end developers who take ownership of HTML/CSS standards and tools. I've taken the first step of documenting CSS formatting standards on my company's wiki and adhering to them in my own work. That's a start, but for standards to be useful, they must be enforced. As senior interaction designer, I have the clout to make that happen, and I've made sure that the few junior designers elsewhere in the company are aware of the standards and the expectation that they follow them. I'm now in the process of educating the developers about them. This is an easy sell—it's just another language. They already "get it."

One thing to be aware of, however, is those auto-formatters I mentioned. Even before I put the standards in place, I was cleaning up every style sheet I touched, simply because it made them easier to work with. Very recently, I began to notice that occasionally a style sheet that I was sure I had already fixed was messed up again. I checked the blame in the VCS and discovered that, yes, a developer had made a change to the file, which was valid, but at the same time changed a lot of the formatting. Upon asking him about it, he realized that as a habit, before saving a file, he always uses the keyboard shortcut that invokes the auto-formatter in his IDE. Eclipse was applying its default formatting rules, which don't match the standards I put in place. We can fix that by either changing the rules or setting the formatter to ignore CSS files.

WHITESPACE

Whitespace refers to spaces and tabs. Either one can be used for indentation of lines of code, but it's important that you pick one and stick to it. The argument against tabs is that a special character must be used to represent a tab and that character may differ from one editor to another. Spaces, therefore, are less likely to result in issues. If there's an argument for using tabs, I suppose it's that they're easier. When you use spaces, you have to set a specific number of spaces and make sure that everyone is using the same number. Most editors will allow you to set them up to automatically insert a certain number of spaces when the tab key is pressed. I strongly suggest that you ask your developers what they use for whitespace and do the same.

COMMENTS

I already explained the importance of commenting your code in Chapter 4, but I should also point out that there are any number of ways to format comments. While you don't necessarily have to be as strict about comments as with the code itself, you should probably put in place some ground rules. In his *"Principles of Writing Consistent, Idiomatic CSS,"* Nicolas Gallagher suggests the following:

- Place comments on a new line above their subject.
- Keep line length to a sensible maximum (e.g., 80 columns).
- Make liberal use of comments to break CSS code into discrete sections.
- Use sentence-case comments and consistent text indentation.

This is a good starting point. The way you treat comments may also depend on the tools you use. One feature I really like in Espresso is its ability to organize styles into groups. It provides a tree view of the style sheet, called the Navigator, which can be quite helpful on large products. It does this using its own comment syntax to denote the beginning and end of a group, as follows:

```
/* @group GroupName */

.aStyle {
    padding: 5px;
}
.anotherStyle {
    margin: 10px;
}

/* @end */
```

Because I'm using Espresso and have encouraged the other designers to do the same, I've included this as part of our formatting standards, and I've created some additional rules around it:

- Groups shall be separated by two blank lines.

- A single line shall separate a style from the opening and closing group comments.

```
/* @group GroupName1 */

.aStyle {
    padding: 5px;
}

/* @end */



/* @group GroupName2 */

.anotherStyle {
    margin: 5px;
}

/* @end */
```

In fact, now that I think about it, most of the formatting rules I've introduced about comments have been derived from this feature. Comments placed outside of a style show up in the Navigator, whereas comments written inside of styles do not. So, I write most comments inside of the styles they relate to, like this:

```
oneMoreStyle {
    /* Comment about a style. */
    margin: 5px;
}
```

A short comment dealing with a specific declaration can be written to the right of the declaration, such as:

```
. lastStyle {
    font-size: 14pt; /* Comment about a declaration. */
}
```

This avoids breaking up the block of declarations, which I want to be able to quickly scan without interruption. General comments and those dealing with a group of styles are written outside of any styles, and therefore show up in the Navigator. The file commentFormatting.css is an example of these rules, as shown in Figure 6.1.

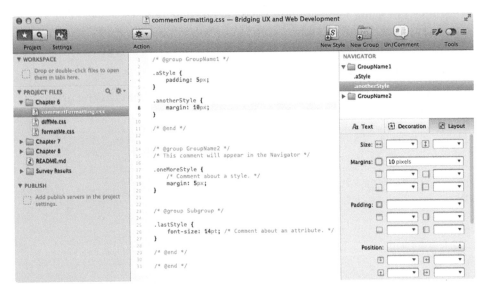

FIGURE 6.1

commentFormatting.css in Espresso

Comments for HTML require slightly different rules, of course, but you get the idea. Some people like to do a lot of fancy formatting, making separators with lines of equal signs and drawing boxes with asterisks. I prefer to keep my comments simple.

```
/* ===================================================================
   This seems like overkill to me.
   =============================================================== */
```

But you, along with your team, can put in place whatever formatting standards suit you and your tools.

FORMATTING CSS

When I began thinking about instituting formatting standards, I was planning on writing them myself. Fortunately, before I invested the time, I became aware of Nicolas Gallagher's Idiomatic CSS project on GitHub. His "reasonable style guide" is based on patterns already in use by most web developers, so they will, for the most part, be familiar and won't require drastic changes to the way you write. However, by codifying them, Gallagher was able to fully consider what makes sense and suggest the better approach where common inconsistencies lay. I've adopted his rules with only a few clarifications and modifications of my own. Here, I include Gallagher's formatting rules unedited. I've found, however, that my workshop attendees tend to misunderstand some of the rules, so I'm providing commentary and examples following each rule to avoid confusion.

1. Use one discrete selector per line in multiselector rule sets.

   It's possible, and very useful, to assign the same style to multiple elements or states through the use of multiple selectors. This can be done by chaining them together with commas like so:

```
.selector1, .selector2, .selector3 {
    padding: 5px;
}
```

   The problem with this format, however, is that it makes it hard to see what selectors a style is being applied to. You have to parse the commas, especially if you have more complex selectors like these:

```
nameSpace .state .button:hover, .nameSpace .state a:hover {
    color: red;
}
```

   So, you see, it can be a challenge to catch the commas. This example only has two selectors. Imagine a rule set with 10 complex selectors. It also makes for really long lines, which is undesirable, let alone soft wrapping the lines and really mucking up the page. So, per the rule, the preferable way to write multiple selectors is with a single line break between each:

```
.selector1,
.selector2,
.selector3 {
    padding: 5px;
}

.nameSpace .state .button:hover,
.nameSpace .state a:hover {
    color: red;
}
```

As you can see, this makes it much easier to understand what the rule is targeting, and it significantly improves your chances of catching an error.

2. Include a single space before the opening brace of a rule set.

    This is an easy one. Instead of `.selector{`, you want `.selector {`. Spaces improve readability.

3. Include one declaration per line in a declaration block.

    This is very similar to the first rule. It'd be syntactically valid to write a style as follows:

    ```
    .selector { float: left; margin: 10px; padding: 5px; }
    ```

    This saves space, but makes it awfully difficult to read. Per the rule:

    ```
    .selector {
        float: left;
        margin: 10px;
        padding: 5px;
    }
    ```

4. Use one level of indentation for each declaration.

    Following the whitespace rule of four spaces, a rule would look like the preceding example, rather than:

    ```
    .selector {
    float: left;
    margin: 10px;
    padding: 5px;
    }
    ```

    Indentation helps us understand the relationships described by code.

5. Include a single space after the colon of a declaration.

    Without the space, you'd have:

    ```
    .selector {
        float:left;
        margin:10px;
        padding:5px;
    }
    ```

    Nobody wants to have to read that. Again, spaces improve readability.

6. Use lowercase and shorthand hex values (e.g., #aaa).

    If you weren't aware, #aaa and #aaaaaa represent exactly the same thing in a hex value. The reasoning here is that where fewer characters will suffice, you may as well avoid the repetition. As for the case, if you're trained in typography, you'll already understand that setting a word in ALL CAPS makes it stand out in your text. There's no reason to hijack attention to color values.

7. Use single or double quotes consistently, preferably double quotes (e.g., `content: ""`).

    Either will work, syntactically speaking, but double quotes are more common. The most important thing is to be consistent.

8. Quote attribute values in selectors (e.g., `input[type="checkbox"]`).

    It'll work without the quotes, but including the quotes is "more correct."

9. Where allowed, avoid specifying units for zero values (e.g., `margin: 0`).

    Dimensions and text sizes can be specified in many different unit types. If a value is zero, however, the unit really doesn't matter, and if it doesn't matter, you shouldn't include it.

10. Include a space after each comma in comma-separated property or function values.

    For example, when specifying a font family, you can include a list of preferred fonts in order of most to least preferred:

    ```
    font-family: helvetica,arial,sans-serif;
    ```

    versus

    ```
    font-family: helvetica, arial, sans-serif;
    ```

11. Include a semi-colon at the end of the last declaration in a declaration block.

    Browsers understand that the end of a CSS rule is the closing brace, so, technically, you don't need the semi-colon on the last declaration. However, if someone later adds a declaration after the last one without realizing that the semi-colon is missing, the last two rules become invalid, and browsers will ignore them.

12. Place the closing brace of a rule set in the same column as the first character of the rule set.

    In unruly code, you'll find the closing brace all over the place:

    ```
    .selector {
        margin: 10px;
        padding: 5px;
        }
    .selector {
        margin: 10px;
        padding: 5px;}
    ```

    Keeping it in line with the first character of the rule set makes it easier to see that a rule is closed:

    ```
    .selector {
        margin: 10px;
        padding: 5px;
    }
    ```

13. Separate each rule set by a blank line.
Say it with me: "Spaces improve readability." For instance:

```
.selector1,
.selector2,
.selector3 {
    padding: 5px;
}
.nameSpace .state .button:hover,
.nameSpace .state a:hover {
    color: red;
}
```

versus

```
.selector1,
.selector2,
.selector3 {
    padding: 5px;
}

.nameSpace .state .button:hover,
.nameSpace .state a:hover {
    color: red;
}
```

DECLARATION ORDER

Now we may be getting to a level of anal-retentiveness that you don't want to indulge in, but for anyone who cares, I'll elaborate. Whereas the order of the rule sets within a style sheet is important to the cascade, the order of the declarations, aside from browser-specific ones, has no bearing on their application in a rendered page. Even so, I've been grouping my declarations based on their effects and then ordering them based on relative importance. For example, there's a massive difference between an element that's `position: absolute` and one that's `position: relative` (which is the default). So, if my rule set has a `position` declaration, I want it at the top where I'll immediately see it. Likewise with the `float` declaration. Directly following these will be any declarations affecting positioning of the element, such as `top` and `margin`. Then I'll have declarations that affect size, and finally those that are merely for appearance (e.g., `color` and `background`).

Gallagher gets into a number of exceptions that you may want to consider, and he provides advice on accounting for preprocessors like Sass. You can find his *"Principles of Writing Consistent, Idiomatic CSS"* on GitHub at *https://github.com/necolas/idiomatic-css#comments.*

MORE TOOLS?

I mentioned that developers employ auto-formatters, and such things do exist for CSS. Some of the editors mentioned in Chapter 5 have some CSS formatting built in or available as plugins. You'll find a number of CSS formatters freely available on the web. Just paste in your code, select the options that you want from a handful of dropdown menus, press a button, and voilà, you have nicely formatted CSS. The best one of these, by far, is ProCSSor.com. And while it does a great job and is free, I prefer to have a native application. As it happens, ProCSSor is also available in the Mac App Store. Try out the website, and if that works for you, you might want the application. I don't run all of my files through it, because it employs a lot of the exceptions Gallagher covers without the option to turn them off. If it were just a little more configurable, I'd make it part of our official development process. That said, I do use it if I'm opening a style sheet for the first time. It gets most of the formatting the way I want it, and there's a lot less for me to fix manually.

FIGURE 6.2

ProCSSor

If Coda is your tool of choice, the Coda PHP and Web Toolkit provides ProCSSor as a plugin. There are similar formatters online for HTML, but nothing like ProCSSor, I'm afraid. I don't particularly care to run all of my company's front-end code through a random website, so I'll wait for some enterprising person to capitalize on the opportunity.

One other tool, which isn't an auto-formatter but bears mentioning, is CSS Lint. The tool checks syntax and validates the CSS against a set of rules, looking for problematic patterns and signs of inefficiency. That happens to be the topic of Chapter 7, so we may as well sling this tool on our belt with the others.

Table 6.1 CSS Formatters

Tool	Developer	Platform	URL
ProCSSor	HyperText Assembly	Web, Mac	*www.procssor.com*
Coda PHP and Web Toolkit	Mario Fischer	Mac	*www.chipwreck.de/blog/?p=723*
CSS Lint	Nicholas C. Zakas and Nicole Sullivan	Web	*http://csslint.net/*

EXERCISE 2: FORMAT AND DIFF

This exercise is going to utilize the file comparison tools we reviewed in Chapter 5 to test your understanding of the CSS formatting standards we just covered.

1. There are two files in the Chapter 6 folder titled formatMe.css and diffMe.css. Open formatMe.css in your editor of choice.

2. This document has a bunch of formatting bugs that I encounter regularly in style sheets created by other designers. Your mission, should you choose to accept it, is to fix the style sheet to meet Nicolas Gallagher's guidelines.

3. When you have finished, diff your file. Open your edited version of formatMe.css and diffMe.css in a file comparison tool. I suggest placing formatMe.css on the left. diffMe.css is a perfectly formatted file. Also, make sure the application is set to include differences in whitespace.

4. How did you do? Did you notice that the very first rule set was indented by tabs rather than spaces? Did you catch the capitalized hex value? More importantly, do you see how much better the file looks when it's consistently formatted? My eyes have been trained to notice discrepancies when I scan a page. That means I'm more likely to notice real errors, but only if I'm looking at a page that follows the formatting standards.

At the end of the day, your guiding principle in developing your own standards is to format code for use by people. There are many things you can do to reduce the size of your CSS, and if that's important for your project, you can run your style sheet through a minimizer (ProCSSor can do that too) before you go live. When you're working, you want your code to be as easy to read and understand as possible. Design your formatting standards with this in mind.

Are you warmed up now? Are you ready to get down and dirty with code? Then grab your garden tools and follow me to Chapter 7. OOCSS awaits!

OOCSS

What is the greatest benefit of using Cascading Style Sheets (CSS)? Let me rephrase that. What *should be* the greatest benefit of using CSS? There are many benefits, to be sure, but the fundamental purpose of CSS is *reuse*. We separate the physical characteristics from an object and give them a name. Then we use that name to assign the same set of physical characteristics consistently to multiple like objects. It's the same concept that's used in formatting text in a word processor. You don't want to have to set the font, size, and style of every heading and subheading in your document, so you create styles that can easily be applied repeatedly. If you decide later that you want to use a different font for the heading, you simply change the style, and all of the headings are automatically updated to match. CSS gives us the same convenience over almost every detail of the visual display. If reuse is the greatest benefit of CSS, then why is it we so often do things that keep it from working that way?

Designers tend to write CSS haphazardly. Just as a developer may implement the first UI that comes to mind if not provided a specification, so too will a designer write CSS off the top of his head without considering the best way to do it. And what do we end up with? We have a style sheet (or five) that's a mile long. We have roll-of-the-dice inheritance. We edit a style having no idea how it'll actually manifest in the browser, and even if it does what we hoped, we can't be confident that it didn't mess up some other element elsewhere in the application. We end up with selectors that are so specific, in order to take precedence over others, that they can't be reused at all. And so we end up writing the same type specifications, the same colors, the same positioning and dimensions, and the same drop shadows over and over. When it comes time to make a system-wide change, we have to seek out each style that's applying that shade of blue or that amount of padding, and apply the same change repeatedly. There's a better way, and it's called object-oriented CSS (OOCSS).

GROUND RULES

Before we get into the specifics of OOCSS, let's lay out a few ground rules. Two of these were already brought up in Chapter 4, but they're worth repeating here.

1. No embedded styles!

   We want to externalize our visual specifications in our style sheet. This gives you the most flexibility to affect change down the road for two reasons. First, styles defined in the HTML take precedence over those in a style sheet, so they can't be overridden without use of the !important modifier. We want to save that for emergency situations only. Second, HTML doesn't always remain as HTML. It may get chopped up into little bits and pieces of JavaScript used to dynamically generate page content. That's going to be a lot more difficult to find, let alone make changes to, than your style sheet. So, do yourself a favor, and just say no to embedded styles.

2. IDs for developers, classes for designers.

   Developers often reference IDs in their code. They don't usually have to reference classes. We can do almost anything we have to do with classes, rarely having to target IDs. Since there's a natural division of interest, let's just go ahead and formalize it. We'll avoid potential conflicts, and in the case that we do have to cross over the line, we'll do it warily and with intent.

3. Use sprites.

   This one, I haven't yet mentioned. If you already know what I'm talking about, you can skip on to the next section. If you don't know what sprites are and why you should use them, hang out here with me a bit. The term comes from early videogame graphics. You can read Dave Shea's original 2004 article introducing the technique on "A List Apart" *(http://alistapart.com/article/sprites),* but I'll give you the basics.

   Let's say we have a button on our page that we're using a graphic for. I know this has fallen out of fashion with everyone going flat, but it's still a good example. The button should have a hover state to reinforce that it's an interactive component. It should have a pressed state to provide feedback when the user clicks it, and it may need a disabled state. There may be other states and variations as well, but these are enough for our example. Each of these states requires a different graphical treatment, so you now have four graphics. Let's also imagine that we have two versions of this button: a red one and a green one. That makes eight graphics. If you implement the button as an <img> element in the HTML, you have to switch it using JavaScript. That's going to require a handler for the mouseover event, another for the mouseout event, yet another for the `mousedown` event, and a fourth for the `click` event. That's going to be a lot of JavaScript and a lot of DOM manipulation. It's also going to be outside of your control, unless you're planning on becoming a full-blown front-end developer. And, unless you preload the graphics, requiring additional JavaScript, the first time the user encounters each of those states, there will be a hiccup as the browser calls the server and requests the graphic for the new state.

There's a much better way to do this. Exercise 3 will demonstrate. You're welcome to follow along with the Button Sprite Example in the GitHub repository. If this concept is completely new to you, I suggest writing your own HTML and CSS as we go.

EXERCISE 3: USING SPRITES

1. First, combine all of your button graphics into a single, flat file. Set it up as a grid. I prefer to use columns for each object and rows for states of an object. I've included my Photoshop file in the repository. The sprite_button.png file was exported from it.

FIGURE 7.1

Button Sprite.psd

2. Rather than using an `<img>` element, you can insert a `<button>` and assign the graphic to it as a `background-image`. In spriteExample.html, you'll see that I've set up two divs with the class `buttonContainer`, and each of those contains two button elements that will become the buttons. I've structured it this way so I can present two rows of buttons. The top row has active buttons and the bottom row has disabled ones. I've added `go` and `stop` classes to distinguish between the two colors. Finally, the `disabled` attribute is added to put them in the disabled state.

Please note that in some cases, I've had to break lines of code unnaturally for them to fit the printed page. In such cases, the break is indicated by this character: ⌐

```
<!DOCTYPE html>
<html lang="en">
    <head>
        <meta charset="utf-8">
        <title>Button Sprite Example</title>
        <link rel="stylesheet" href="spriteExample.css" ⌐
          type="text/css" />
        <!--[if lt IE 9]>
        <script src="http://html5shim.googlecode.com/⌐
          svn/trunk/html5.js"></script>
        <![endif]-->
    </head>
    <body>
        <div class="buttonContainer">
            <button class="go"></button>
            <button class="stop"></button>
        </div>
        <div class="buttonContainer">
            <button class="go" disabled></button>
            <button class="stop" disabled></button>
        </div>
    </body>
</html>
```

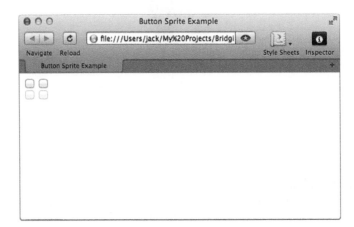

FIGURE 7.2

HTML before any CSS is applied

3. Now, let's turn our attention to spriteExample.css. I've set the background of the page to gray. .buttonContainer spaces the buttons off from the edges of the screen and spaces the two rows from each other with a 50-pixel margin. overflow: hidden is included because all of the div's contents will

be floated, and this forces it to expand to the size it should be to contain the buttons, rather than collapsing down and taking up no space on the page at all. `.buttonContainer button` floats the button elements so that they can sit beside each other and spaces them apart 50 pixels.

```
html {
    background: gray;
}

.buttonContainer {
    margin: 50px;
    overflow: hidden;
}

.buttonContainer button {
    float: left;
    margin-right: 50px;
}
```

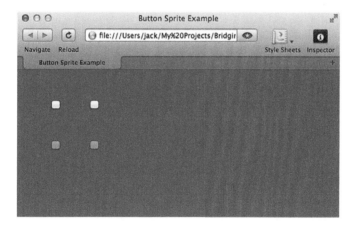

FIGURE 7.3

Initial CSS, before styling the buttons

4. To create the buttons, we first have to set the height and width of the divs. My graphic happens to be 50 × 50 pixels, so we should set the `button` height and width to the same. Get rid of the default button styling added by browsers by setting `border` to `none`. Now we add sprite_button.png as the background. Since both the green and red graphics are in the same file, we only have to set the background image once.

```
button {
    height: 50px;
    width: 50px;
    border: none;
    background: url(sprite_button.png) no-repeat;
}
```

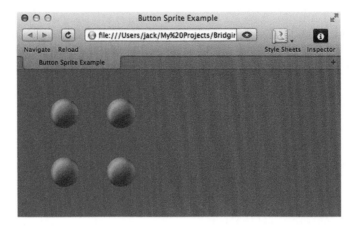

FIGURE 7.4

Styled buttons without differentiation

5. Since the button divs are set to the dimensions of the button graphic, only the default state of the green button shows. Let's add the `.stop` selector to distinguish between the green and red buttons. We'll just move the background image 50 pixels to the left by setting the x value of `background-position` to a negative value. This reveals the red version of the button within the div.

```
.stop {
    background-position: -50px 0;
}
```

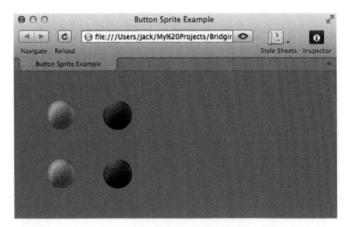

FIGURE 7.5

Green and red buttons

6. Now we can use the CSS pseudo-classes `:hover` and `:active` to change the *y* value of `background-position`, again subtracting 50 pixels at a time, to reveal the corresponding areas within our sprite. While I'd love to be

able to use `background-position-x` and `background-position-y`, saving having to set the *x* value for every state, Firefox doesn't support them.

```
button:hover {
    background-position: 0 -50px;
}

.stop {
    background-position: -50px -50px;
}

button:active {
    background-position: 0 -100px;
}

.stop {
    background-position: -50px -100px;
}
```

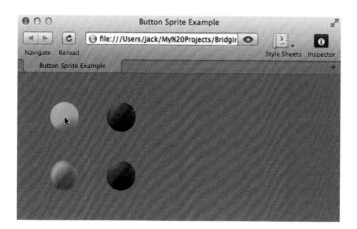

FIGURE 7.6
Hover states enabled

7. Finally, we'll add a selector for the `disabled` attribute. We want this one to come last in our style sheet so that it'll take precedence over the `hover` and `active` selectors.

```
button[disabled] {
    background-position: 0 -150px;
}

.stop[disabled] {
    background-position: -50px -150px;
}
```

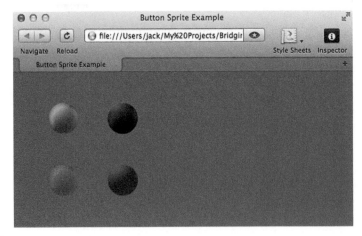

FIGURE 7.7

Disabled states added

This will improve performance, as you only have to call the server once to get the graphic when the page loads, rather than making four separate calls. It'll also improve maintainability, since it's done in CSS rather than JavaScript. It improves flexibility, because you can make changes with CSS. Finally, the designer maintains full control over the behavior. This approach is desirable for the majority of graphics utilized in the UI. Think about an application with dozens of icons and multiple sizes and states for each. Combining them all into a single graphic file will significantly reduce the number of calls to the server, which translates directly to better performance.

To improve maintainability, I document all of the sprites I create on our wiki, naming the states, recording the pixel coordinates, and cross-referencing the graphic in the application to the Photoshop file from which it was created.

TWO PRIMARY PRINCIPLES OF OOCSS

OOCSS was first presented as an approach by Nicole Sullivan at Web Directions North 2009 in Denver, CO. Unfortunately, I wasn't tuned into the cutting edge of web development at that time. I was making all of the mistakes I described in the introduction to this chapter, and I was having a hard time meeting deadlines because of them. I started separating my CSS declarations into simpler rule sets that could be applied more flexibly. I thought I was onto something. Then, in March 2011, Brian Cavalier, a former coworker, gave my company a presentation on OOCSS. He explained very clearly what I had unknowingly been trying to do. I was excited to see my ideas not just validated but significantly improved upon. I was able to immediately take his lessons and apply them to the work I was doing. Our front-end code made a quantum leap in maintainability, and, since then, I've been shouting the praises of OOCSS to anyone who will listen. It all comes down to three primary principles. Wait, doesn't that section title say "Two Primary Principles…"? Yes, well, we'll start out with the original two principles that Sullivan presented. Then we'll add Cavalier's third principle in Chapter 8.

Separate structure and skin

Think about a frame-construction house. All of the rooms are built the same way. Walls are formed by a series of vertical boards (studs) connected to each other with horizontal boards (wall plates). These are the structure. They give the entire house a shape with particular dimensions and act as the base for applying covering material, such as wall sheathing and siding on the exterior, and wallboard and paint on the interior—the skin. A web page also has both structure and skin, but it isn't a neat division between HTML and CSS, as you may be thinking. CSS can manipulate both the structure and the skin. There are declarations that affect position on the page, such as `top`, `left`, `margin`, `position`, and `float`. Declarations like `height` and `width` specify dimensions. These are all structural in nature, defining the shape of a web page just as framing defines the shape of a house. Once that structure is in place, it can be skinned with `color`, `border`, `font`, `background`, and many other declarations that don't affect the structure. Due to the fluidity of HTML, there are some declarations that can affect both, such as `line-height`. As you begin to understand the OOCSS approach, you'll form your own mental model as to what qualifies as structure and skin.

When creating classes, keep them separated into structure classes and skin classes. This will allow you the flexibility to reuse your structure classes on elements that are consistently sized and placed on multiple screens, but may look different. At the same time, you can reuse your skin classes to consistently apply visual styling to any structural element. For example, you may have a footer bar that appears on every page of a site. It's always at the bottom, and it's always the same height. However, depending on the page, it may be different colors. One class defines the footer as being of a certain height on the bottom of the page, and another class defines its color. The classes defining the color can also be applied to the headers without any worry that the headers will end up on the bottom of the page.

You've already seen a simple example of this in Exercise 3. Remember how the `button` style defined the dimensions of the button, whereas the `stop` class and `disabled` attribute were applied to give the button a particular appearance? "Ah, but what about the background image?" you cleverly ask. Isn't that considered skin? Yes, it is, and if we had the green and red buttons as separate sprites, we would want to separate the background image specification into `start` and `stop` classes. However, in this case, since we know that for a 50 × 50 pixel button we'll always be using the same sprite as the background image, it makes sense to specify it once in the structural class. So, you see, this isn't a hard-and-fast rule that must not be broken. Rather, it's a guideline that should be carefully considered and broken when it'll result in cleaner code. The goal is to identify repeating visual patterns and define them as styles that can be applied to multiple elements without breaking your structure.

Separate container and content

The idea here is that an object should look and behave the same regardless of where it's located. If I define `<div class="button">` for use in my footer and later decide that I also want to use it in my header, I should be able to drop it into my header confident that it'll look exactly the same as the button in my footer. I'm embarrassed to admit that I feel a bit hypocritical writing this, as I still struggle to adhere to this principle. CSS makes it so easy for us to write selectors that target an element based on its location in the DOM. I often feel justified in special-casing a style because I know that it's only going to apply in that context. I designed it that way. But, designs change—screens get added and features are morphed and refined. You really need your code to remain flexible. Let's say, for example, that we have buttons in the footer that always line up on the right side. We could write a style like this:

```
.footer .button {
    float: right;
    margin-right: 10px;
}
```

This would cause all of our buttons to line up from the right edge spaced 10 pixels apart from each other. Sometime later, we decide that we want buttons on the right side of our header too. Oh, and we need one button on the left side of our footer. You could duplicate the style for the header and then write a special case for the left-aligned footer button, but that would be silly. What you really should do is create general classes for floating elements left and right and extend the button class to use them:

```
.right {
    float: right;
}

.left {
    float: left;
}

.button.right {
    margin-right: 10px;
}

.button.left {
    margin-left: 10px;
}
```

Now, it doesn't matter whether the button is in the header, footer, or some other element that hasn't been added to the site yet; You know that if you add the `right` class to it, it'll float to the right side of its container and space itself 10 pixels away from whatever it's beside.

Following this principle, we should try not to use descendant selectors:

```
.buttonBar p {...}
li div .icon {...}
```

There should also be very little call for using elements with attached classes in our style sheet:

```
div.footer {...}
p.mainText {...}
```

To really get a handle on these principles, you need to play around with some code. It's time for another exercise.

EXERCISE 4: REDUCE, REUSE, RECYCLE

In this exercise, we're going to use the files in the OOCSS folder within the GitHub repository. Go ahead and open oocss_original.html in a browser or preview it within your editor. I've mocked up a page reminiscent of a blogging application. There aren't any editing controls, and the navigation isn't functional. The only behavior in the page is the hover and active states on the toolbar. All we care about for this exercise is the layout and appearance: the structure and skin. The "original" files are written as would be expected by one untrained in the OOCSS approach. We're going to fix them, making the code OOCSS compliant, while maintaining the appearance of the page.

FIGURE 7.8

oocss_original.html

1. A quick look at the HTML reveals the structure of the page to be quite simple. There are three main divs: one for the toolbar, one for the blog post, and one for the note. Each has been assigned a single identifier class. The toolbar contains divs for each of the tools, and they have been identified with a class as well. The post is semantically organized into an `<h1>` for the title and a `<p>` for the body. The note also contains a `<p>`, but some of its content is wrapped in spans so that it can be styled separately.

```
<!DOCTYPE html>
<html lang="en">
    <head>...</head>
    <body>
        <div class="toolbar">
            <div class="tool">Text</div>
            <div class="tool">Photo</div>
            <div class="tool">Video</div>
            <div class="tool">File</div>
        </div>
        <div class="post">
            <h1>Idiot Tags</h1>
            <p>I love idiot tags...</p>
        </div>
        <div class="note">
            <p>
                <span class="userName">fishstickmonkey</span> ⌐
                liked your post:
                <span class="title">Idiot Tags</span>
            </p>
        </div>
    </body>
</html>
```

2. So, what kind of shape is the CSS in? Open oocss_original.css. Oh, that looks messy. Of course, a large part of the perceived messiness is due to the browser-specific declarations for border radius and background gradients. A lot of that will have to stay. The first thing to do is start looking for repeated declarations. One that jumps out at me right off the bat is the font declaration. You won't often require many of these, and they're typically defined on high-level elements. I see four: two `font` and two `font-family` declarations. The font families are all identical, so let's move them into a single declaration on the `<html>` tag. In so doing, we can delete the two existing `font-family` declarations. The two `font` declarations must be broken down into separate declarations for the remaining `font-size`, `font-weight`, and `line-height` declarations, as follows:

```
html {
    ...
    font-family: Helvetica, "Helvetica Neue", Arial, Geneva, ⌐
      sans-serif;
}

.tool {
    ...
    font-size: 2em;
    font-weight: bold;
    line-height: 50px;
    ...
}

.post h1 {
    font-size: 2em;
    font-weight: bold;
    ...
}
```

3. If you examine the `box-shadow` declarations on the `.tool`, `.post`, and `.note` rule sets, you'll notice that they're identical. That's a lot of duplication. Let's create a `shadow` class that can be assigned to any element to which we want to give a drop shadow:

```
.shadow {
    -moz-box-shadow: 5px 5px 10px rgba(0, 0, 0, 0.75);
    -webkit-box-shadow: 5px 5px 10px rgba(0, 0, 0, 0.75);
    box-shadow: 5px 5px 10px rgba(0, 0, 0, 0.75);
}
```

Of course, we now have to assign the shadow class to the HTML elements:

```
<div class="tool shadow">...</div>
<div class="post shadow">...</div>
<div class="note shadow">...</div>
```

4. The exact same thing can be done to the `border-radius` declarations found on `.post` and `.note`. Pull them out into their own `.corners` rule set and apply the `corners` class to the post and note divs:

```
.corners {
    -webkit-border-radius: 10px;
    -moz-border-radius: 10px;
    border-radius: 10px;
}
```

5. There are two other rule sets in which `border-radius` is being defined: `.tool:first-child` and `.tool:last-child`. These are putting the rounded

corners on the ends of the toolbar without affecting the divs in the center. We won't save lines of code here, but we can be a little smarter. Right now, we have border-radius defined as 10 pixels in three places. One would reasonably expect to be able to change it in the .corners rule set and have it change everywhere. As things stand, one would have to figure out why the corners on the toolbar didn't change, eventually finding the other two locations where border-radius is defined. Let's reverse the way the corners on the toolbar are being defined. Instead of only rounding the outer corners of those two divs, add the corners class to them. Then, change the .tool:first-child and .tool:last-child rule sets to override the border-radius on the inner corners.

```
<div class="toolbar">
    <div class="tool shadow corners">Text</div>
    <div class="tool shadow">Photo</div>
    <div class="tool shadow">Video</div>
    <div class="tool shadow corners">File</div>
</div>

.tool:first-child {
    -webkit-border-top-right-radius: 0;
    -webkit-border-bottom-right-radius: 0;
    -moz-border-radius-topright: 0;
    -moz-border-radius-bottomright: 0;
    border-top-right-radius: 0;
    border-bottom-right-radius: 0;
}

.tool:last-child {
    -webkit-border-top-left-radius: 0;
    -webkit-border-bottom-left-radius: 0;
    -moz-border-radius-topleft: 0;
    -moz-border-radius-bottomleft: 0;
    border-top-left-radius: 0;
    border-bottom-left-radius: 0;
}
```

6. There's one more significant block of code we can get rid of. The toolbar and the note both share the same gradient. Move this to a new .boxGradient rule set and add the boxGradient class to the note div and each of the tool divs:

```
<div class="toolbar">
    <div class="tool shadow boxGradient corners">Text</div>
    <div class="tool shadow boxGradient">Photo</div>
    <div class="tool shadow boxGradient">Video</div>
    <div class="tool shadow boxGradient corners">File</div>
</div>
```

```
div class="note shadow corners boxGradient">...</div>

.boxGradient {
    background: #e1ffff;
    background: -moz-linear-gradient(...);
    background: -webkit-gradient(...);
    background: -webkit-linear-gradient(...);
    background: -o-linear-gradient(...);
    background: -ms-linear-gradient(...);
    background: linear-gradient(...);
    filter: progid:DXImageTransform.Microsoft.gradient(...);
}
```

7. We've found a lot of repeated skin styling, but what about structure?
    Look at the rule sets for those three main divs again. They all have the
    same `max-width`, `min-width`, and `margin`. We want to pull those out and
    stick them in a new `.contentBox` structure style:

```
.contentBox {
    max-width: 90%;
    min-width: 430px;
    margin: 50px auto;
}
```

   `contentBox` now becomes the primary class for these three divs. The original
   identifier divs only have one or two declarations on them now.

```
<div class="contentBox toolbar">...</div>
<div class="contentBox shadow corners post">...</div>
<div class="contentBox shadow corners boxGradient note">...</div>
```

8. The `.tool` rule set shares the same text styling as `.post h1`. To remove
    that duplication, we can put both selectors together. They can easily be
    separated in the future if need be. At the same time, let's get rid of that
    descendant selector. The `h1` should look the same everywhere when it
    has no class.

```
h1,
.tool {
    color: #616161;
    font-weight: bold;
    font-size: 2em;
}
```

9. We're now left with a few odds and ends. We still have a 20-pixel margin
    that's defined for `.post h1`, `.post p`, and `.note p`. We know now that
    those descendant selectors are just trying to trip us up. Don't let them.
    Add `.content` as a new rule. Perhaps it'll do more in the future, but for
    now, it'll just apply the margin.

```
.content {
    margin: 20px;
}
```

10. The very last thing to do is to get rid of the remaining two descendant selectors: `.note p .userName` and `.note p span.title`. The classes are already applied to the spans, so the extra specificity here is worthless.

```
.userName {
    font-weight: bold;
}

.title {
    font-style: italic;
}
```

If you made all of the changes correctly, the file should still look exactly as it did before when rendered in a browser. Under the covers, on the other hand, you have a much cleaner style sheet. It contains fewer lines of code, it's better organized, and the classes are actually reusable. You can check your work by diffing your files against oocss_revised.html and oocss_revised.css.

CREATING COMPONENTS

Now that you understand the two main principles of OOCSS, let's explore the potential of this approach. Remembering that the biggest benefit of CSS is reusability, it only follows that OOCSS should capitalize on it. When a product is developed with an OOCSS approach, you can create components that can be dropped into a page requiring little additional CSS. You may very well be able to build a new screen by copying and pasting code snippets without writing a lick of new CSS. If you utilize design patterns, OOCSS is a perfect compliment. Your pattern library can be extended to include HTML components. You want rapid prototyping? It's conceivable that with such a library, you could go from thumbnail sketch to functional prototype within a matter of minutes.

An excellent example of such a concept in action is Bootstrap, a front-end framework originally developed by a designer and developer at Twitter. Bootstrap has a slew of components, such as navigation bars, pagination controls, breadcrumb trails, and progress bars. Each component has a default setup defined by a single class that can be modified with the addition of other classes. Take their button group component, for example. The `btn` class is what assigns the basic appearance of a button to either the `<a>` or `<button>` element. Wrap two `btn` objects within a `<div>` assigned the `btn-group` class, and they'll form a little button bar where the outer corners are rounded, but the inner edges meet perfectly.

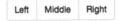

FIGURE 7.9

Bootstrap button group

If you want the buttons to be smaller, you can add the `btn-group-sm` class.

FIGURE 7.10

Small button group

If you'd rather have the buttons stacked vertically, you can replace `btn-group` with `btn-group-vertical`.

FIGURE 7.11

Vertical button group

Add additional classes like `btn-danger` and `dropdown-toggle`, and all of a sudden, you have a colored button that will display a drop-down menu when paired with some additional HTML specifying its content.

FIGURE 7.12

Danger button with a drop-down menu

The system is flexible and simple to use. It's also relatively easy to customize. Bootstrap is very well designed. A lot of thought was given to how each component can be used individually and in concert with other components. It's a good model for anyone who is maintaining a product suite and looking for ways to improve consistency and maintainability.

EXERCISE 5: A PRACTICAL EXAMPLE OF REUSABLE COMPONENTS

In this exercise, we're going to take a look at Amazon.com's homepage. If you're signed in to the site and scroll down, you'll see several rows of products: Related to Items You've Viewed, New for You, Get Yourself a Little Something, etc. Notice that all of the rows are styled the same way. There's a section title with a rule below it. Then there's a series of products arranged horizontally. Each product has a thumbnail image, below which are details such as the title, author, publisher, star rating, price, and so forth, depending on the type of item.

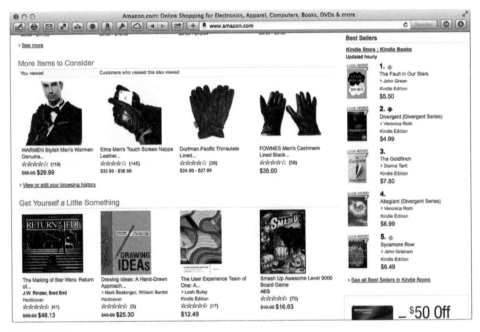

FIGURE 7.13

My homepage on Amazon.com

Turn on your inspector and select one of the items. Work your way up the DOM until you get to the div for the section, which will look something like this:

```
<div class="unified_widget rcm widget small_heading s9Widget ⌐
    s9Multipack" id="ns_1YN9AFOMVEZWOQN7V1XR_10641_Widget">
```

This is the container for the section. It contains an `<h2>` for the title and a series of divs. The div with the `row` class is the one that contains the products. Looking in there, you'll find a bunch of divs and spans that make up each of the products. Each product has the same structure with the same classes applied.

Now look at the right side of the page. There's a column that contains a couple product lists. I see two Best Sellers lists, one with videogames and a second with Kindle books. You may see different lists depending on your purchase history and when you're reading this.

Examine the visual structure of the list. You'll note that it's composed of nearly identical elements. There's a section title. There's a series of products, each with a thumbnail image and, to the right of the image, details about the item. There are some differences. The items are listed vertically, rather than horizontally. The details are to the right of the images, rather than below them. The items are numerically ranked, and the section titles are styled differently. By and large, though, the lists on the side appear to be vertical versions of the horizontal lists. One might reasonably expect, then, that they'd have the same HTML structure. The product lists are obviously reusable components, and a little CSS could change the orientation.

Well, let's take a look. Target one of the products on the side with your inspector. The top element for the list is similar to the top element for the horizontal lists.

```
<div class="unified_widget" ⌐
    id="zgChart_ns_1YN9AFOMVEZWOQN7V1XR_993_">
```

However, you'll notice a couple levels deep, there's a `<table>`. Wait, what? Sure enough, the HTML structure for this list is entirely different than the horizontal lists. Well, surely they're using the same classes. Select the price and make note of the class assigned to it. This is a price from the vertical list:

```
<strong class="price">$3.49</strong>
```

This is a price from a horizontal list:

```
<span class="s9Price red t14">$19.96</span>
```

Even though the text is being styled exactly the same, the classes aren't shared at all. We can do better than that. Let's give Amazon a hand. In your GitHub repository, you'll find a folder named 5. Amazon Example. Open amazon_original.html. I've done a lot to simplify this file for our purposes.

I've extracted the Get Yourself a Little Something section, keeping the ancestral elements that contain it. In the process, I externalized all of the embedded CSS in the file embedded.css. Nasty embedded CSS. We hates it, yes we do, my precious. I've also added a bunch of comments indicating what the classes are controlling. This will make it easier for you to understand what's going on without hunting through Amazon's style sheets, which I did run through ProCSSor to make readable. I grabbed the images that we need, stuck them in the Graphics folder, and created references to them in the code. Finally, I pulled out all of the JavaScript. We're just dealing with layout, so the JavaScript is superfluous to this exercise.

FIGURE 7.14

Get Yourself a Little Something

Here's what we're going to do. First, we'll convert the code to be more OOCSS compliant without changing the layout. Then, we'll add the CSS that will allow it to change orientation.

Step 1

To get started, make a copy of amazon_original.html. You'll want to keep that file around for reference as you make changes to your copy. Now, create a new CSS file and link it into your copy of the HTML file. We don't want to have to work within the existing files, so give yourself a clean slate. For the sake of reference, I'm naming my files amazon_inProgress.html and amazon_inProgress.css.

Step 2

Find `<div class="s90therItems" style="float: left; width: 100%">`. Everything from here up controls placement of the entire widget on the page. For now, we just have to worry about the arrangement of the content within the individual product blocks. As you'll see, they haven't been designed for flexibility. You may want to enter a couple line breaks as a visual indicator of where we're working. Rather than editing a product, let's build a new one, creating our own, simplified HTML structure. We can copy the actual content from the first product into it as we go. We'll start by creating a container for the product:

```
<div class="productBlock"></div>
```

Step 3

Look again at the visual structure of the information. Right away, it's clear that there are two significant objects that we can model in the code: the image and the text. Now, in the original code, you'll find the image wrapped in the same `<a>` as the product title. That works fine when the title is immediately below the image. However, if you want to put the image and information side-by-side, you can't have the image wrapped by the same element as one detail in the information. Let's set up a structure that we know we can reorient later:

```
<div class="productBlock">
    <div class="imgBlock"></div>
    <div class="detailBlock"></div>
</div>
```

Step 4

With that simple structure in place, we can start copying in the content from the first product in the list. Copy the `<img>` element into the `imgBlock` and wrap it in the anchor tag that's needed to link to the product page:

```
<div class="imgBlock">
    <a href=""><img src="Graphics/philipsHue.jpg" style= ⌐
        "margin-top: 23px"></a>
</div>
```

It's not necessary to specify the dimensions of the image because it isn't being resized. It'll default to its actual size, so I removed that. I left the inline style setting the margin, however, because it's the only way to vertically center the graphic. The product thumbnails are variable heights, so the top margin has to be calculated and written directly into the HTML. This will be done in JavaScript.

Step 5

Now fill out the `detailBlock`. Take an inventory of everything that may be displayed, and add a div for each one. Throw the title, wrapped in its anchor, into the `title` div. The `credit` and `descriptor` divs can either always be included and left empty, as I've done here, or just left out completely when they don't apply. The empty divs have no effect in the display. Remember that all of this is being generated by Amazon's Content Management System (CMS), so it'd just leave them out. I'm creating container divs for the rating and price because those are composed of multiple elements.

```
<div class="detailBlock">
    <div class="title"><a href="">Philips Hue Connected Bulb ↵
        Starter Pack</a></div>
    <div class="credit"></div>
    <div class="descriptor"></div>
    <div class="ratingBlock"></div>
    <div class="priceBlock"></div>
</div>
```

Step 6

Now fill out the `ratingBlock` and `priceBlock` divs. Their rating/reviews component is already designed well, so the only changes I made to it were to move the parentheses inside the anchor (I just like it better that way) and add my own generic class for hiding the label. As an aside, you should take a minute to examine how they're displaying the stars. It's a really nice use of sprites.

```
<div class="ratingBlock">
    <div class="s9Stars s9Stars_4_0"></div>
    <span class="reviews">
        <a href="">( 7<span class="hidden"> customer ↵
            reviews</span> )</a>
    </span>
</div>
```

The `listPrice` span is another element that could be left out altogether when not applicable:

```
<div class="priceBlock">
    <span class="listPrice"></span>
    <span class="price">$269.99</span>
</div>
```

If you're tracking your changes in your live preview, it should currently look like Figure 7.15. Even though we haven't written any styles for our new classes, some styling is already being applied by the existing style sheets. In fact, notice that we're using the price class used in the vertical lists that I pointed out earlier.

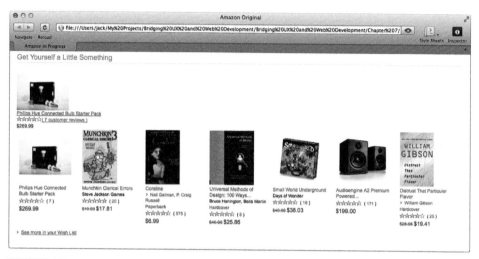

FIGURE 7.15

New, unstyled product

Step 7

Now we need to write the CSS that will make our new component play nicely with others. Currently, productBlock is a block element that takes up the entire width of the page. We need it to sit side-by-side with the other products. In your new CSS file, add the following rule set:

```
.productBlock {
    float: left;
    width: 14.285714285714286%;
    font-size: .916em;
    line-height: 14px;
}
```

Where did these values come from? We have to float the div so that it'll sit beside other divs. The width was calculated by dividing 100% by 7—the number of products we want to display in a single row. Note that this is another value that's going to be programmatically determined based on the width of the browser and the number of products that will fit at the time the page loads, but we'll just set it for the seven products I included in the example. The font-size comes from the style that was originally used on the text elements, and I'm setting a base line-height that I took from the calculated value reported in my inspector.

That got the `productBlock` displaying in line with the others, but there's still some work to do. Add the following rule set:

```
.imgBlock {
    height: 135px;
    margin-bottom: 4px;
}
```

The product images are always 135 pixels tall, and there's a 4-pixel space between the image and the title. With that, we're really, really close. There's just some detailed textual styling left to do.

FIGURE 7.16

Almost there

Step 8

Now we need to grab a lot of declarations from the old CSS. The easiest way to do this is with your browser developer tools. Style the `title` and `descriptor` divs as follows:

```
.title {
    font-size: 12px;
    color: #004B91;
}

.descriptor {
    color: #666;
}
```

Style the `price` and `listPrice` spans as follows:

```
.price {
    font-size: 14px;
    line-height: 1.286em;
    letter-spacing: .025em;
    color: rgb(153, 0, 0);
}

.listPrice {
    color: rgb(102, 102, 102);
    text-decoration: line-through;
}
```

Add some spacing to the `ratingBlock` **div** as follows:

```
.ratingBlock {
    margin-top: 3px;
    margin-bottom: 3px;
}

.reviews {
    margin-left: 6px;
}
```

To style the link, I have to use descendant selectors to increase specificity. Without them, some other style in one of Amazon's sheets takes precedence.

```
.productBlock div a:link {
    text-decoration: none;
}

.productBlock div a:hover {
    text-decoration: underline;
}
```

And to hide anything that needs hiding, we have the generic `.hidden` rule set:

```
.hidden {
    display: none;
}
```

With that, the new product block looks like the original. The wrapping is slightly different, and there's a good reason for that, but we'll take care of it in a minute.

FIGURE 7.17

Match

Step 9

Now that you have one product done, reimplement the other six using the same structure. When you're done, it should look like Figure 7.18.

FIGURE 7.18

All products replaced

Step 10

Not bad, but we missed something important. There's nothing to space the `productBlock` divs apart from each other. I had planned to do this by putting left and right margins directly on the `productBlock` divs, but that makes the percentage widths too wide. Interior padding also messes up the widths. So, we have to reintroduce a wrapping div that I originally removed. Add the `inner` div just inside of the `productBlock` div as follows:

```
<div class="productBlock">
    <div class="inner">
        ...
    </div>
</div>
```

Propagate this additional div to the other products, and add the following rule set to the style sheet:

```
.inner {
    margin-right: 7px;
    margin-left: 7px;
}
```

At last, we have a much simpler HTML page that exactly matches what we started with. And while the simplification of the code is a worthy endeavor, it isn't the reason we started this exercise. It's time for a little CSS magic.

FIGURE 7.19

Back where we started

> ## INTERLUDE
>
> If you want to check your work before proceeding, you can compare your files with amazon_revised.html and amazon_revised.css. We're now going to purposefully employ a descendant selector with dramatic results. We're going to create a modifier class that has no styles directly assigned. Rather, it creates a namespace we can use to indicate a vertical list. All of the selectors we use now will begin with the namespace, so they'll only apply in the vertical context. It's another powerful way to get a lot of reuse out of existing components, but it goes against the second principle of OOCSS. This is one case where understanding the rules allows us to judiciously break them to great benefit.

Step 11

Add the class `verticalList` to the container for the entire list as follows:

```
<div class="unified_widget rcm widget small_heading s9Widget ⌐
    s9Multipack verticalList" id="ns_OGKCVSCJ2KMWY6BGH2P2_12630_Widget">
```

This is the only change we'll make to the HTML.

Step 12

Reposition the list container as follows:

```
.verticalList {
    float: right;
    width: 300px;
}
```

This sets the list against the right edge of the window and restricts its width. Your live preview looks bad now, but we'll get it sorted out in a hurry.

Step 13

Most of the work is going to be done by resetting the product blocks. We'll cancel the float, causing them to stack. We'll also override the percentage widths and set top and bottom margins to space them apart. We don't need the inner div for that this time.

```
.verticalList .productBlock {
    float: none;
    clear: both;
    width: 100%;
    margin-top: 10px;
    margin-bottom: 10px;
    overflow: hidden;
}
```

We now have the products laid out nicely in a column, but the details are still underneath the images.

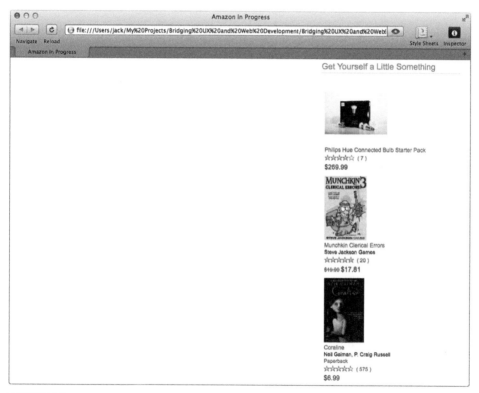

FIGURE 7.20

Stacked

Step 14

Since we broke the image and details into separate divs, we can float them to get them sitting side-by-side:

```
.verticalList .imgBlock,
.verticalList .detailBlock {
    float: left;
}
```

However, the longer titles still cause the detail blocks to wrap down under the images. We'll fix that by reducing the widths of the images and the detail blocks.

Step 15

Height is no longer the controlling factor for the `imgBlock` element, so we can remove the height from it and specify width instead. We should also add a right margin to space off the details.

```
.verticalList .imgBlock {
    height: inherit;
    width: 100px;
    margin-right: 10px;
}
```

Step 16

Here's the ugly bit. The `margin-top` used for vertically centering the graphic is no longer desired. Since it's an embedded style, the only way to cancel it in the style sheet is to use the `!important` designation. Again, ideally there would be no inline styles, and this wouldn't be necessary, but we're dealing with some predefined code here, rather than something we built from scratch. We can live with it, but try to avoid causing this kind of situation in your own code. To finish off the `img`, assign a maximum height and width to shrink the image to a size more suitable for the vertical layout, as follows:

```
.verticalList .imgBlock img {
    max-height: 100px;
    max-width: 100px;
    margin-top: 0 !important;
}
```

Step 17

Finally, by adding a maximum width to the detail block, we'll cause the longer titles to wrap, rather than wrapping the entire block:

```
.verticalList .detailBlock {
   max-width: 175px;
}
```

FIGURE 7.21

Job's done!

And that's it. We've created a class that switches from a horizontal layout to a vertical one. To see the magic in action, watch your live preview while you delete the `verticalList` class from the HTML and paste it back in. Abracadabra! You can check your work against amazon_vertical.html and amazon_vertical.css. For another check, paste your style sheet into CSS Lint. It should find no errors and give you a single warning about that `!important` designation.

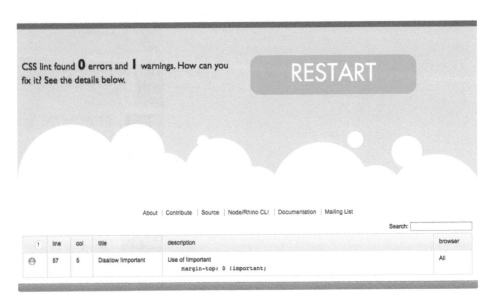

FIGURE 7.22

CSS Lint

Hopefully, this exercise has clearly illustrated the power of well-architected HTML components matched with flexible OOCSS. But why stop there? At the beginning of this chapter, I hinted at a third principle. In Chapter 8, I'll show you how OOCSS can replace JavaScript.

Owning Behavior

8

In Chapter 7, I gave you the first two principles of OOCSS—the principles that were originally espoused by Nicole Sullivan:

- Separate structure and skin.
- Separate container and content.

Brian Cavalier and John Hann introduced a third principle in their presentation *OOCSS for JavaScript Pirates:*

- Separate identity and state.

I'm not referring to the `id` attribute. We already know that we don't want to use that. "Identity," in this case, refers to the base class, which is typically going to be the structure class, and any skin classes that are being applied to it. These classes define the default state of an object. Additional object states can be declared with the addition of state classes. For example, think back to the buttons in Exercise 3:

```
<div class="buttonContainer">
    <button class="go" disabled></button>
    <button class="stop" disabled></div>
</div>
```

We used the `button` element to define the structure, the button's size and placement, as well as its default skin, which was the background graphic. If `go` and `stop` are simply variants of a button, they'd be considered skin classes, but let's say that they're actually two states of the same button. It's a toggle that changes from red to green or back again when pressed. In that case, `stop` is a state class that will be assigned to the button when it should be in the red state and removed when the button should be green. Therefore, `button` is the identity of a button and `stop` is its state. Of course, there are other states defined by the :hover and :active pseudo-classes, as well as the disabled state, and they all have to act in concert with the stop and go states.

This third principle enables us to significantly reduce the amount of JavaScript used to implement UI behaviors. Reducing JavaScript will improve performance, improve maintainability, and give you, the designer, more direct control over the behavior of your product. I can demonstrate with a simple form.

EXERCISE 6: THE OTHER FIELD

In the GitHub repository, preview form_original.html. In the rather limited Favorite Dessert menu, there is, of course, an option for "Other." Upon selection, it'll display a field in which to enter the dessert that wasn't listed. This is a very common design pattern, and if you take a look at the HTML, you'll see an implementation that I often encounter. First, note the select element:

```
<select name="dessert" onclick="test()">
```

FIGURE 8.1

form_original.html

It has a name that can be targeted by the JavaScript. It also has an onclick handler that will call the JavaScript at the top of the page every time a selection is made. Now examine the <tr> containing the "Other" field:

```
<tr id="otherRow" style="display: none;">
```

The row has an ID, and by default, it's hidden with an inline style. Nasty, embedded style. It burns us! Well, we'll deal with that in a minute. Let's look at the JavaScript in the <head>:

```
<script>
    function test() {
        var otherRow=document.getElementById('otherRow');
        if (document.querySelector('[name="dessert"]').value == ⌐
            'other') {
            otherRow.style.display='';
        }
        else {
            otherRow.style.display='none';
        }
    }
</script>
```

When a selection is made in the `dessert` menu, it runs this function. The function checks the value of the menu. If "Other" is selected, it searches the DOM for `otherRow` and sets its style attribute to `display: ;`, causing the row to show in the page. If any other value is selected, it searches the DOM for `otherRow` and sets its style attribute to `display: none`, removing it from the page.

FIGURE 8.2
The Other field

This works, but allow me to show you a more enlightened approach. Preview form_revised.html. Sure, it looks and behaves exactly the same as the previous file, but take a peek under the covers. There have been no changes made to the `select` element. What about the `<tr>` containing the "Other" field? A-ha! Instead of an ID and that pesky inline style, it has a single class assigned:

```
<tr class="otherRow">
```

Looking at the style sheet, you'll find this rule set:

```
.otherRow {
    display: none;
}
```

Okay, so we're still hiding the row by default, but we're doing it in the style sheet through class assignment, rather than an embedded style. That's important, but it's only a small part of the story. We need to dive into the JavaScript to understand what's going on here:

```
<script>
    function test() {
        var simpleForm=document.querySelector ⌐
            ('[name="simpleForm"]');
        if (document.querySelector('[name="dessert"]').value ⌐
            == 'other') {
            simpleForm.classList.add('other');
        }
        else {
            simpleForm.classList.remove('other');
        }
    }
</script>
```

There's a fundamental difference here. Can you see it? The function is still called in the same way, but instead of digging into the DOM to find otherRow, it's looking for simpleForm, the name on the top-level form element. Instead of writing an inline style to show or hide a specific element, it's simply adding a state class (other) to a high-level, structural object, or removing the same. Returning to the style sheet, we'll find this rule set:

```
.other .otherRow {
    display: table-row;
}
```

This selector utilizes the other state class to show the row containing the "Other" field. When the form is in the other state, the field shows; otherwise, the field is hidden.

At face value, you may not think that this is much of an improvement. We really haven't reduced the amount of code that's being used. Yes, the JavaScript can find the top-level form element more quickly than the row, which is deeper in the DOM, but it's an imperceptible difference. So, what's the big deal? This is a very simple example to allow a simple explanation. The value comes with scale, as you'll see in the final exercise.

But before we bring this plane in for landing, there's one other significant revelation. Think back to what we did in exercise 5. Remember that verticalList class we used as a descendant selector to reorient the product list from horizontal to vertical? It should be apparent now that we were using a state class. We placed the list in a vertical state. So, as it turns out, we weren't breaking the OOCSS principles at all—we were just using one that I hadn't taught you yet.

EXERCISE 7: ECONOMY OF SCALE

Before we get started, let me say one word about JavaScript libraries. Most front-end developers these days use them, and with good reason. It's a lot easier to build complex behaviors with a library than by writing JavaScript from scratch. That said, introducing jQuery now would add complications to this book that aren't necessary for the point I'm making. For this reason, I'm sticking to some very simple, basic JavaScript in these exercises. I encourage you to find out what libraries your team uses and learn how they add and remove classes or otherwise implement behaviors. As always, your context will greatly affect your approach, but I hope that my lesson will be applicable regardless. With that understanding, bring on the code!

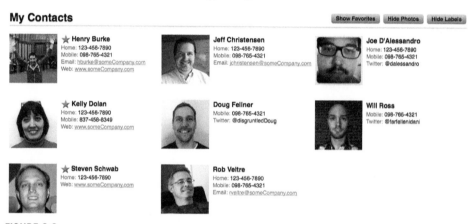

FIGURE 8.3

Contact list

In the GitHub repository, preview contactList_complete.html. I'm not going to claim that this contact list is the epitome of interaction design, but it'll suffice for our exercise. The list has three features, represented by the buttons in the top-right corner. You can choose to only show the contacts marked as favorites (the ones with stars) or show everyone. You can choose to show or hide the photos, and you can show or hide the labels. Each button works as a toggle.

FIGURE 8.4

Photos and labels are hidden

FIGURE 8.5

Only favorites are shown

Now preview contactList_incomplete.html. The only apparent difference is that the toggle buttons display labels for both states at once. Of course, clicking them does nothing. The incomplete versions of the HTML and CSS files have all of the structure and skin styling in place, but they're missing the behavioral styling. Your mission, should you choose to accept it, is to hook up the buttons so that they'll show and hide the correct elements on the page. I encourage you to give it a try without my help. The JavaScript is already written, but with placeholders for classes, so even if you don't know JavaScript, you can probably figure out what has to go where. Of course, you're welcome to follow along with me as we work through it.

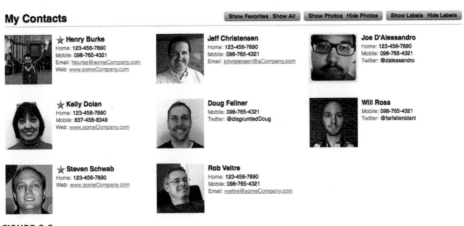

FIGURE 8.6

contactList_incomplete.html

Step 1

The first thing to do is decide on our states. There are six states, two for each toggle, but since they're all binary, we only need to define a single state class for each toggle and then set up our default state. Let's say that by default, everything is hidden. The presence of our state classes will indicate that corresponding content should be displayed. That said, we want everything to be shown when the screen first loads, so we want to begin with our state classes in place.

Add state classes to the top-level div as shown here:

```
<div class="contactList photosOn labelsOn all">
```

So, the presence of `photosOn` will cause the photos to display. The presence of `labelsOn` will cause the labels to display. The presence of `all` will cause all of the contacts to display, rather than just the favorites.

Step 2

Next, wire these classes up in the style sheet. Find `.infoBlock .label`. Hide the labels by adding `display: none;`:

```
.infoBlock .label {
    color: #838383;
    display: none;
}
```

You'll see the labels disappear in your live preview. Now do the same thing with `.photoBlock`:

```
.photoBlock {
    width: 125px;
    height: 125px;
    overflow: hidden;
    margin-right: 10px;
    display: none;
}
```

Hmmm. Without the photos, all of the text is overlapping. We'd better fix that.

FIGURE 8.7

Whoops

Step 3

Find the following rule set and comment it out:

```
.infoBlock {
    position: absolute;
    top: 0;
    left: 135px;
}
```

That only applies when the photos are displayed. We'll have to make it conditional, which we'll do in a minute, but for now, just disable it. Now, our text isn't overlapping, but it's still spaced apart enough to include the photos. Let's reclaim that space.

Find .contact, and change the minimum width to 250 pixels:

```
.contact {
    position: relative;
    float: left;
    margin-bottom: 40px;
    min-width: 250px;
}
```

We still need to keep the original width for when the photos are displayed, so add the following rule set:

```
.photosOn .contact {
    min-width: 400px;
}
```

It'll be applied immediately, since we already have photosOn in place. Feel free to comment that out until later.

Step 4

We've hidden the labels and the photos. Next, hide the contacts themselves:

```
.contact {
    position: relative;
    float: left;
    margin-bottom: 40px;
    min-width: 250px;
    display: none;
}
```

Step 5

At this point, everything is hidden, but we want the favorites to be displayed when we aren't in the all state. So, add a rule set to show them:

```
.favorite {
    display: inherit;
}
```

That overrides the `display: none;` we added in Step 4.

Step 6

Our default state is done. Now we need to add the rule sets that show everything when the three state classes are applied (as they are now). Add the following rule sets in the appropriate places within the style sheet:

```
.all .contact {
    display: inherit;
}

.photosOn .photoBlock {
    display: inherit;
}

.labelsOn .infoBlock .label {
    display: inline;
}
```

You'll also want to go back and reenable the rule sets we commented out. Add the `.photosOn` selector in front of `.infoBlock` so that it'll only be used in the `photosOn` state:

```
.photosOn .infoBlock {
    position: absolute;
    top: 0;
    left: 135px;
}
```

Step 7

Your live preview should now be back to looking the way it did when we started. Behind the scenes, all of the states are in place. Let's turn our attention to those buttons. We need to hide the labels that should be hidden. We're going to need identity classes on the label divs. Let's use `hide` and `show` for the corresponding labels:

```
<div class="button toggleFavorites" onclick="toggleFavorites()">
    <div class="l"></div>
    <div class="c hide">Show Favorites</div>
    <div class="c show">Show All</div>
    <div class="r"></div>
</div>
<div class="button togglePhotos" onclick="togglePhotos()">
    <div class="l"></div>
    <div class="c show">Show Photos</div>
    <div class="c hide">Hide Photos</div>
    <div class="r"></div>
</div>
```

```
<div class="button toggleLabels" onclick="toggleLabels()">
    <div class="l"></div>
    <div class="c show">Show Labels</div>
    <div class="c hide">Hide Labels</div>
    <div class="r"></div>
</div>
```

The classes for favorites seem backwards, but think of it as hiding and showing nonfavorites. Now create the corresponding CSS that will utilize those classes. Add the following to the bottom of the style sheet:

```
.togglePhotos .hide,
.toggleLabels .hide,
.toggleFavorites .hide,
.photosOn .togglePhotos .show,
.labelsOn .toggleLabels .show,
.all .toggleFavorites .show {
    display: none;
}
```

This list of selectors hides the `hide` labels when not in the default state and then uses the state classes to hide the `show` labels when the states are in effect. Of course, at the moment, all of the button labels are hidden. We need one more rule set to show the `hide` labels in the default state when the state classes are applied:

```
.photosOn .togglePhotos .hide,
.labelsOn .toggleLabels .hide,
.all .toggleFavorites .hide {
    display: inherit;
}
```

Step 8

All that's left is to wire up the buttons. Turn back to your HTML file and look at the JavaScript. All of the state classes are being applied to the `contactList` div, so that's the only element that the functions have to target. The `init` function stores the location of `contactList` in a global variable. Replace `.myClass` with `.contactList`. Then in the three toggle functions, `myClass` should be replaced with the state class that applies to each function. For example, in the `toggleLabels` function, `myClass` should be replaced with `labelsOn`. In the end, your JavaScript should look like this:

```
<script language="javascript" type="text/javascript">
    var contactList;

    function init() {
        contactList=document.querySelector('.contactList');
    }

    function toggleLabels() {
        contactList.classList.toggle('labelsOn');
    }

    function togglePhotos() {
        contactList.classList.toggle('photosOn');
    }

    function toggleFavorites() {
        contactList.classList.toggle('all');
    }
</script>
```

And with that, your buttons now toggle each of the states.

CLASSY CODE

You see how it has been implemented using state classes. Now consider what would have to happen for the same behavior to be implemented via direct DOM manipulation with JavaScript. For every button click, the JavaScript would have to walk the DOM, searching for matching IDs and writing style attributes directly into multiple HTML elements. I think you'll agree that such an approach now seems clumsy and verbose. The elegance of swapping state classes limits the complexity of the JavaScript, making troubleshooting and revisions much easier. Reducing DOM manipulation will improve performance, and the fact that the behavior is now defined primarily in the style sheet means that it's implemented and controlled by the same people who are specifying it.

What does this mean, then, for your process and documentation? I have some suggestions for you:

- *Design your code.* While you're at the sketching/wireframing stage, you already have most of the information you need to design your class structure. You can actually label your wireframes with structure class names. You can list your states and assign classes to those as well. Skin class names will come later as the visual design is worked out.

- *Include state classes in your UI specifications.* When you deliver specifications to the developers, you should include instructions detailing what state classes should be assigned to which elements under what conditions. I include these instructions as comments within the code, too, where the developers will see them in context as they turn my HTML into a JSP. The wiki is another excellent place to document your classes, especially if that's where the developers document their design.

- *Hold a code review.* More than any other part of your code, state classes are where the developers should have some input. They may have ideas on how to improve your code design in ways you haven't thought of. As Brian Cavalier put it, the state classes represent a contract between the view (HTML and CSS) and view controller (JavaScript), so it's important for this to be designed collaboratively.

Don't wait; act now! You don't have to wait for a new project or a UI "refresh" to start putting these approaches into practice. Whenever you open a style sheet for editing, give it a quick formatting clean-up. As you edit styles, take a few extra minutes to make them OOCSS compliant. Your code will be that much better going forward, and it'll save you time in the long run.

Looking Toward the Horizon

9

You've filled your toolbox, standardized the formatting of your CSS, created reusable OOCSS components, and started moving behavior out of JavaScript and into your CSS. Your team is working together effectively, and your products are looking and behaving more and more like your design specs. You, my friend, have reached the summit of your career. I guess it's time to kick your feet up and coast.

Hah! You know better than that. Before taking my leave, I'd like to suggest some directions you may want to explore as you seek your next adventure in web design. There are always new tools, processes, and approaches to improve your work. Never stop learning.

CSS PREPROCESSORS

As I've been telling you, CSS is a relatively simple language. It's simplicity is in large part responsible for its popularity. However, that simplicity also means that it's missing some abstractions that can make your code even more flexible. Just as we can use OOCSS to modularize your styles for optimal reuse in your HTML, preprocessors can bake reusability into your style sheets. A preprocessor adds a new layer of script with its own syntax to CSS, providing abilities that CSS doesn't have natively—abilities such as defining variables that can be used throughout a style sheet. Of course, in so doing, the style sheet becomes unreadable by browsers, as it now has a lot of unrecognizable script in it. That's where *preprocessing* comes in. The additional script is only there for your benefit, affording you some conveniences in the authoring of your style sheets. It must be interpreted by software that understands it and translates it to compliant CSS before being rendered in a browser.

Once you understand how to use them, preprocessors can help you to be more efficient and flexible with your style sheets, but heed this warning: preprocessors are not replacements for OOCSS practices and well-architected CSS. I'm only just beginning to explore how to judiciously integrate them. If you try to fix your CSSpaghetti with preprocessing alone, you're likely to end up with preprocessed spaghetti. Yuck. Your problems will remain; they'll just be abstracted a level, and that will make troubleshooting them even more difficult. Preprocessors are all about convenience within your style sheets. After processing, your style sheet should still reflect the best practices this book has focused on. To achieve that is going to take some, uh, noodling.

There are currently three popular preprocessors: Sass, Less, and Stylus.

Feeling Sassy

Sass, a catchy acronym for Syntactically Awesome Style Sheets, is the creation of Hampton Catlin, Nathan Weizenbaum, and Chris Eppstein. It comes in two flavors of syntax. The original, indented SASS syntax eschews much of CSS's native formatting of braces and semicolons for visually cleaner indentation and line breaks. For example, where a block of CSS looks like this:

```
.buttonContainer {
    margin: 50px;
    overflow: hidden;
}

button {
    height: 50px;
    width: 50px;
    border: none;
    background: url(sprite_button.png) no-repeat;
}
```

The SASS syntax would be:

```
.buttonContainer
    margin: 50px
    overflow: hidden

button
    height: 50px
    width: 50px
    border: none
    background: url(sprite_button.png) no-repeat
```

To my taste, this is a little too foreign, like the first time I tried real Indian curry. It won't likely take you too long to adjust to it, and you may come to like it, but the strangeness of it is an impediment to adoption for those of us who are already CSS experts. If that's where Sass stood, I might not give it the time of day. But, its creators developed a second syntax, dubbed Sassy CSS or SCSS. It uses the same formatting as CSS, so a valid CSS file can be converted to a valid SCSS file simply by changing the extension to .scss. That's more to my liking.

So, what makes Sass so tasty? It contains the following ingredients.

Variables

Variables alone make Sass a very attractive compliment to your newfound OOCSS approach. Typically, when designing a website or application, you develop a consistent graphic design consisting of a color scheme, a typographic hierarchy, and some form of grid or layout template. In other words, throughout your design, you have colors that are used repeatedly, type styles that are used repeatedly, and dimensions that are used repeatedly. Looking at your style sheet, you'll find the same hex values repeated all over the place. If you decide to change a color, you have to search for and replace every instance in which that color is used. It'd be a lot cleaner if you could define that color once, give it a name, like "errorRed," and then use the name in any rule that specifies the color. If you decide later that errorRed will have more impact if it's a bit brighter, all you will have to change is the one hex value where you originally specified the color. Sass will ensure that the change is written in everywhere the name was used.

That's a variable, and that's exactly what Sass offers you. It's employment looks like this:

```
$errorRed: #b11e13

.errorText {
    color: $errorRed;
    font-style: italic;
}

.errorBar {
    background-color: $errorRed;
    height: 25px;
}
```

Once your .scss file is processed into a .css file, the preceding block will look like this:

```
.errorText {
    color: $b11e13;
    font-style: italic;
}

.errorBar {
    background-color: $b11e13;
    height: 25px;
}
```

This is an error bar!

This is error text!

FIGURE 9.1

$errorRed

As you can see, you'll end up with CSS just as you'd write it now, but you have the added convenience of defining variables to make your coding easier.

Mixins

Variables are great for single values like colors, but what about repetitive chunks of CSS, such as shadows and gradients, where you have to include browser prefixes, resulting in large rule sets? Mixins work like variables, but represent a block of rules, rather than a single value. They also allow you to define arguments—variables that you can fill in where the mixin is used. For example, you might define a mixin like this:

```
@mixin shadow($h, $v, $blur, $color) {
    -moz-box-shadow: $h $v $blur $color;
    -webkit-box-shadow: $h $v $blur $color;
    box-shadow: $h $v $blur $color;
}
```

The mixin's name is `shadow`, and rather than enter values, I've included variables that are defined as arguments in the parentheses following the name. Now, to add a shadow to a rule set elsewhere in the style sheet, you'd be able to do this:

```
.contentBox {
    height: 100px;
    width: 300px;
    margin: 30px auto;
    background-color: #5c90aa;
    @include shadow(5px, 5px, 10px, rgba(0, 0, 0, 0.75));
}
```

The generated CSS would then be this:

```
.contentBox {
    height: 100px;
    width: 300px;
    margin: 30px auto;
    background-color: #5c90aa;
    -moz-box-shadow: 5px 5px 10px rgba(0, 0, 0, 0.75);
    -webkit-box-shadow: 5px 5px 10px rgba(0, 0, 0, 0.75);
    box-shadow: 5px 5px 10px rgba(0, 0, 0, 0.75);
}
```

FIGURE 9.2

Mixed-in shadow

Imagine all of the lines of code you could avoid having to write. But wait, there's more.

Extends

I often end up with rule sets that are shared by a bunch of classes. Even putting line breaks between each selector, they can become unwieldy. Extends allow you to extend an existing rule set through selector inheritance. Let's say you have a standard, inline message style, and you want to make a yellow version for a caution message and a red version for a warning. You might write CSS that looks something like this:

```
.message,
.caution,
.warning {
    padding: 5px;
    border: 1px solid #333;
    background-color: #cecece;
}

.caution {
    background-color: #eeee74;
}

.warning {
    font-weight: bold;
    background-color: #ea6a6a;
}
```

Using Sass, you'd get exactly that once processed, but could also write it as follows:

```
.message {
    padding: 5px;
    border: 1px solid #333;
    background-color: #cecece;
}

.caution {
    @extend .message;
    background-color: #eeee74;
}

.warning {
    @extend .message;
    font-weight: bold;
    background-color: #ea6a6a;
}
```

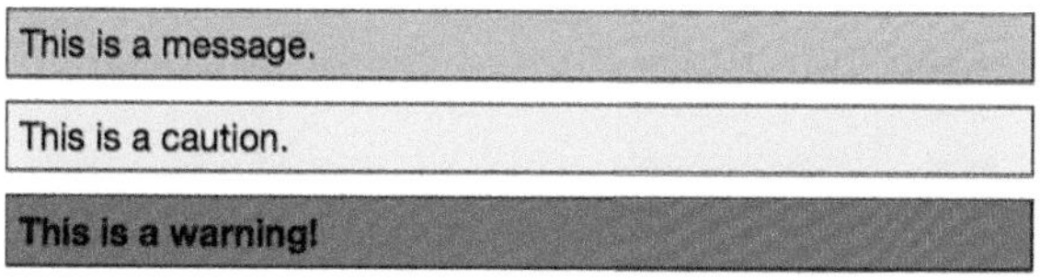

FIGURE 9.3

Extended messages

This is a very simple example, so it doesn't offer much benefit over the standard CSS. But, if you extrapolate this out to a style that has a list of 10 or more complex selectors on a single rule set, you may find it to be a bit cleaner and easier to understand what gets what from what. Be careful, however, as extensive use of extends may just result in a lot of indirection and style sheet bloat. You need to think hard about what makes sense to do as an extend, and what would make more sense as an OOCSS helper class. Even in this simple example, would we be better off making `message` a base class that is extended by the `caution` and `warning` classes?

```
.message {
    padding: 5px;
    border: 1px solid #333;
    background-color: #cecece;
}

.caution {
    background-color: #eeee74;
}

.warning {
    font-weight: bold;
    background-color: #ea6a6a;
}
```

This OOCSS approach requires that you add two classes to an element for a caution or warning message in your HTML, whereas the Sass extends allow you to use a single class. However, the OOCSS approach allows `.caution` and `.warning` to be defined independently from `.message`, which means they can be used to modify other classes as well. Maybe you'll have a distinct `.modalMessage` rule set that defines a pop-up dialog, which also must be adapted to caution and warning versions. So you see, it's a bit tricky. Don't fall into the trap of designing for your current convenience at the expense of reuse and true extensibility of your CSS architecture.

Nesting

I'm less interested in this particular Sass feature, but it bears mentioning. Sass will allow you to nest styles within other styles. When they compile, the nested styles become rule sets with descendant selectors. And that's why I find this capability of less value. Per OOCSS, descendant selectors are something we want to stay away from. But, I suppose I ought to provide an example.

If you must use descendant selectors, this is how to conveniently implement them with Sass:

```
ul {
    font-family: "Helvetica Neue", Helvetica, Arial, sans-serif;
    color: gray;
    li {
        font-size: 12px;
        font-weight: normal;
        color: black;
    }
    li.title {
        font-size: 14px;
        font-weight: bold;
    }
}
```

When processed, it'd convert to the following:

```
ul {
    font-family: "Helvetica Neue", Helvetica, Arial, sans-serif;
    color: gray;
}

ul li.title {
    font-size: 14px;
    font-weight: bold;
}

ul li {
    font-size: 12px;
    font-weight: normal;
    color: black;
}
```

This is the title.
- This is just a list item.
- This is just another list item.

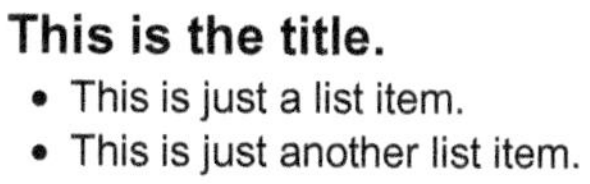

FIGURE 9.4

Nested descendants

There's a lot more Sass can do—enough to deserve its own book—and Dan Cederholm has written a good one. If you're interested in having a go with Sass, pick up a copy of *Sass for Web Designers* from A Book Apart.

Less is more

Less, loosely standing for Leaner CSS, was designed by Alexis Sellier and heavily influenced by Sass. In turn, the SCSS syntax was inspired by Less. It's no surprise, then, that Less has a similar feature set. Just like Sass, Less gives you variables, mixins, extends, and nesting. The syntax is slightly different— variables are defined with the at sign (@) rather than a dollar sign ($), for example—but the capabilities are the same. Nevertheless, Less offers a good bit more functionality in the way of operations and functions.

Numbers, colors, and variables can all be used in mathematical operations. For example, `height: 100% / 2;` is going to give you a height of 50%. That's not so useful by itself, but combined with variables and a long list of functions (*http://lesscss.org/functions/*), you could, for example, code your style sheet to compute its own color values, rather than defining every possible color explicitly. This could be useful anywhere that you have many variations of a base color, such as bevels, shadows, gradients, borders, alternating striped rows, etc. Perhaps hovering over elements on the page changes their color values by increasing their saturation by 20% and lightening them by 10%. You could figure out what that would be for each color in Photoshop and then copy and paste the hex values into your style sheet. Or you could let Less do the work for you:

```
@baseColor: #b04d46;
@saturation: 20%;
@lightness: 10%;

div {
    height: 100px;
    width: 100px;
    background-color: @baseColor;
}

div:hover {
    background-color: lighten(saturate(@baseColor, @saturation), ⏎
        @lightness);
}
```

After processing, the resulting CSS looks like this:

```
div {
    height: 50px;
    width: 50px;
    background-color: #b04d46;
}

div:hover {
    background-color: #d85a51;
}
```

FIGURE 9.5

Base color versus hover

This example is just one square, but imagine having 20 of them, each a different color. If you decided later that the saturation was increased too much, and you wanted to drop it to a 15% increase, you wouldn't have to go back into Photoshop to figure out 20 new hex values. All you'd have to do is change that single percentage value, because you were smart enough to make it a variable too. In doing so, you're not just optimizing your code, but the development process itself. Hey, you're really getting the hang of this.

Stylus

Stylus is the youngest of the three preprocessors, so it is influenced by both Sass and Less. It takes the original, minimalist approach of the SASS syntax to an entirely new level, but accepts standard CSS syntax also. To me, this sounds like a nightmare from the standpoint of formatting standards. If anything goes, how can you hope to catch mistakes? Like its older siblings, Stylus has variables, mixins, nesting, etc. It also has the operators and functions of Less. It goes several steps further, adding conditionals (if/else), hashes, and other gobbledygook that surpasses my programming know-how, so please excuse me for not providing examples. If you ever reach a point at which you're applying this level of code sophistication in your style sheets to true benefit, let me know. I'd be interested to know what you're doing with it.

Preprocessors are another tool available to you, but a tool should never be used for its own sake. Doggedly using a hammer to pound in a screw isn't going to help anyone. Using a preprocessor without first knowing exactly what benefit you intend to get from it is more likely to make things harder for you than to solve anything. So, before resolving to use one, consider why you need it. A lot of the problems you face will be solved with well-architected OOCSS, so you may not need a preprocessor. Are you going to significantly benefit from the use of variables to define and maintain your web style guide? Will the power of computing color variations improve the efficiency of your development process? Remember that a decision to use preprocessors is one that affects your entire team. Everyone who is going to edit the CSS will have to commit to learning and using the preprocessor. You'll have to adapt your processes. It is not a trivial decision, and you should certainly get buy-in from your entire development team before adoption.

Oh no, not the terminal!

If you decide to start playing with preprocessors, that means you'll be writing your CSS in a file without a .css extension. That won't be the file that you reference into your HTML, of course. So you may be thinking, "This all sounds cool, but how do I see what I'm working on, and how do I actually process the file to get usable CSS?" Well, there are commands that you can enter into the terminal, but I don't want to touch that any more than you do. Thank goodness, there are tools!

Most of the editors I went over in Chapter 5 support both Sass and Less through plugins. I'm afraid Espresso falters on this point. The Sass sugar only supports the SASS syntax. Coda, on the other hand, supports both preprocessors natively and will support Stylus with a plugin. Another plugin will even allow Coda to compile. One editor I hadn't mentioned before, because it is more a JavaScript IDE than it is an HTML and CSS editor, is WebStorm from JetBrains. I have to give it credit here, though, as it provides code completion, formatting, syntax highlighting, and automatic compilation for all three preprocessors.

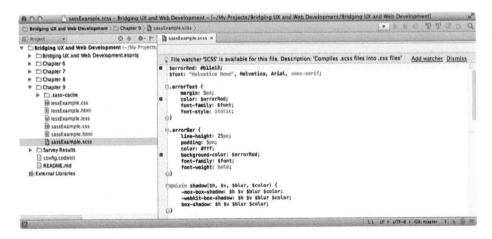

FIGURE 9.6

WebStorm

Then there are applications solely devoted to the task of compiling. They typically watch for a file to change, so when you save a .scss file in your editor, the compiler will notice and automatically generate a new CSS file, writing over the last version. Most of them will also automatically refresh your browser, so it's almost as good as a live preview. CodeKit, created by Bryan Jones, compiles Less, Sass, Stylus, and several other types of files. It provides a slew of options that can be set on a file-by-file basis, and it will automatically refresh browsers across devices. Another application that covers all three is LiveReload, by Andrey Tarantsov. Koala, by Ethan Lai, has a simpler feature set, but covers Sass and Less, is cross-platform compatible, and is free of charge (donations accepted). Hammer only handles Sass, but it offers a lot of other functionality that's worth checking out. Other free options are Scout for Sass and SimpLESS for Less.

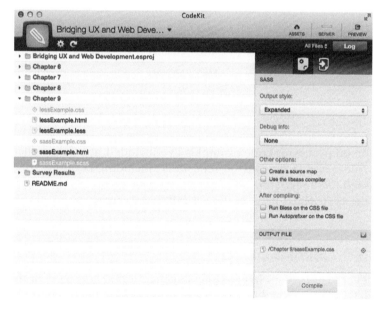

FIGURE 9.7

CodeKit

Table 9.1 Preprocessors

Tool	Developer	Platform	URL
Sass	Hampton Catlin, Nathan Weizenbaum, Chris Eppstein		*http://sass-lang.com*
Less	Alexis Sellier and core team		*http://lesscss.org*
Stylus	LearnBoost		*http://learnboost.github.io/stylus/*
WebStorm	JetBrains	Mac, Windows, Linux	*http://www.jetbrains.com/webstorm/*
CodeKit	Bryan Jones	Mac	*https://incident57.com/codekit/*
LiveReload	Andrey Tarantsov	Mac	*http://livereload.com/*
Koala	Ethan Lai	Mac, Windows, Linux	*http://koala-app.com*
Hammer	Riot	Mac	*http://hammerformac.com*
Scout	Mutually Human	Mac, Windows	*http://mhs.github.io/scout-app/*
SimpLESS	KISS	Mac, Windows	*http://wearekiss.com/simpless*

All of the preprocessor code examples I've included here are available in the Chapter 9 folder within the GitHub repository, including both the unprocessed and processed CSS files. You can play around with them, test them out with a couple of the tools listed here, and we'll call that Exercise #8.

JAVASCRIPT LIBRARIES

Have you ever imagined an interaction, sketched it out, specified all the behavior details, and upon explaining it to a developer, been rebuffed because he or she didn't know how to do it and didn't have the time to figure it out? "That sounds difficult, and difficult isn't in our estimates." That situation is exactly what drove me to jQuery. I was certain there was a better way to implement a particular feature of an application, but it was only going to happen if I did a little work during my design phase to prototype it—not to create an animated demonstration, mind you, but to prototype it using a technology by which it could eventually be implemented. Sure, I had taken some online courses in JavaScript once upon a time, but I never used it enough to really understand it. It never stuck. JavaScript libraries (also referred to as frameworks) take the complexity of JavaScript and package it up into powerful, easily understood functions that simplify common tasks.

There are a slew of them to choose from (e.g., Prototype, MooTools, Dojo), but jQuery is king of this particular hill. It's by far the most popular library, which means it has the most tutorials, examples, companion frameworks, and helpful resources. All you have to do is Google something like "jQuery set variable from select," and you're guaranteed to get a page full of results that will tell you exactly how to do it with the cleanest jQuery code. I can't write jQuery from scratch (yet), but I sure can copy and paste. That's all I needed to create a prototype that was able to convince my development team that we could implement the UI I was proposing on budget—and by the way, no, it won't cause horrendous performance problems, and yes, it even works in IE 6. Heh. If you ever run into me during a conference reception, ask me why I'm still developing for IE 6. It's a great story.

But this isn't the place for that story, nor is this the book to teach the ins and outs of jQuery. It's a magical land that I'm still exploring myself. I hope that when you feel ready, you'll join me there. When you do, be sure to check out jQuery's companion frameworks. jQuery UI specializes in common interactions like drag and drop, resizing, selecting, and sorting. It provides specialized, customizable widgets like date pickers and progress bars, and makes animated effects a breeze to implement.

FIGURE 9.8

jQuery UI website

That said, I also want to impress upon you two warnings. First, code you have copied off the web isn't necessarily good code or the best way to do it in your team's technology stack. It may be completely outdated. Listen to your mother when she says, "Don't pick that up; you don't know where it's been." When I proved the viability of my solution to my development team with a jQuery prototype, it was just that: a prototype. I worked with my developers to refine it, and I went through a legitimate code review with the team before it was ready for production implementation. Don't get delusions of grandeur. If you think that you know JavaScript better than your developers, you can expect the same reaction that you would likely have if a developer claimed to know more about UI design.

The second warning is that many JavaScript libraries come "complete" with UI components. They make it easy to implement a layout grid or accordion fold or [insert conventional widget here]. These components come with their own prejudices about how things should be done. I've seen designers employ them because they are quick to implement. I've seen software teams choose to use them in production for the same reason. But they're not always easy to adapt. They may not fit your particular application well, and your hands may be tied when you end up wanting to modify the way they look or behave. For expediency in one build cycle, you may end up damning yourself for the life of the product. Make sure that you and the rest of your team understand the difference between the prototype and the goal for the design, both from the perspective of the user experience and architecturally. When it comes to JavaScript frameworks, these are often inextricably intertwined.

Table 9.2 JavaScript Libraries

Tool	Developer	URL
jQuery	The jQuery Foundation	http://jquery.com
Prototype	Prototype Core Team	http://prototypejs.org
MooTools	MooTools Development Team	http://mootools.net
Dojo	The Dojo Foundation	http://dojotoolkit.org

HARNESS UP YOUR APP AND RIDE

CSS gives you a lot of control over the UI, but there's a lot more to a web application than what we see in the browser window. The back end involves servers and databases. There may be third-party components and integrations with external systems. That's a lot of overhead to maintain on every developer's build environment, and it's just not practical to do so. However, certain features won't work without those pieces hooked up. You may not be able to navigate to a particular screen, or if you can get there, it may not display any data. It's awfully difficult to adjust the styling of a page if you can't actually see it. Furthermore, there are any number of states and conditions that must align to result in the screen you're looking at. A simple example is an error dialog. To get an error dialog to display on screen in a running application, you must cause that error to occur. That may be as simple as trying to save something without giving it a name, or it could involve a combination of user group permissions, system administrator settings, and the time of day. In situations like this, there are a couple of things you can do.

The first option is to bug a developer. You have to schedule a time that he or she can set you up with exactly what you require to access the part of the application you need to get to. The developer may have to manually enter data into your database so that content populates on your screen. Or, the developer may have to give you access to a VM that's set up with an external system. If you have to do this once or twice, maybe it's not a big deal. Maybe the developer won't mind taking the time to help. But if it's a common occurrence— if you're repeatedly having to get special assistance to complete your tasks—it's going to slow you down, and it's going to slow down the developers who have to help you. This is an option, but not an optimal or sustainable one.

So, what's the alternative? During the design phase, work with your developers to identify areas of the application that will cause these types of problems. Let the developers make the call as to how they want to approach it, but make sure they understand what you're going to need to be able to do. They may decide that it's worthwhile to spend a little time upfront to create a test harness. A test harness is a bit of code that runs separately from the application. It will contain only what's necessary for you to see what you need to see.

Let's say, for example, that you have a graphical status display in your application for some external systems that your application monitors. Your company even installed the systems so that your team would be able to develop the interfaces with them. However, you have to implement the status displays for every possible state each of the systems can be in, and you don't have any way of creating those states in the systems yourself. It might be worthwhile for one of the developers to stub out a web page with some buttons on it that will transmit the various states to your status display. Then, all you would have to do to test your work on the status display is press a button and see if it responds as you expect it to.

In simpler situations, you may even be able to create your own test harnesses. For an application I was working on, I had a lot of modal dialogs that I had to implement. The trouble was, I was working on the HTML and CSS before the guts that would open the dialogs were hooked up. So, I built myself a simple test harness using a little jQuery. All I had to do was change a class name on the modal dialog framework, and it'd load the correct content from an HTML file. Once I had it rendering the way I wanted, I could take that HTML file, change its extension to .jsp, and check it into Subversion. I've held onto that test harness, and as we've revised the application, I've used it whenever I've had to add a new dialog. The time I spent building it has saved a lot of time in the long run.

Why not try your hand at creating a simple test harness now?

EXERCISE #9: TEST HARNESS

Let's pretend that you're designing a status panel for a critical system. The software is built on a client/server model to support offline use. The application runs in a web browser, and it typically accesses a database on a server. However, when the network is down, it can access a local database directly on the client machine. This allows it to store data in the interim, and once the server is back, the client database syncs up with the remote database. To make sure the user is aware of what's going on, you have to create a status panel that indicates the current state of the client's connection to the server, as well as the amount of storage space utilized on the client.

Look in the "Test Harness" folder in Chapter 9 of the GitHub repository. Notice that I've included the jQuery library. We're going to go ahead and take advantage of it in this exercise. Preview statusPane_incomplete.html. It looks like Figure 9.9.

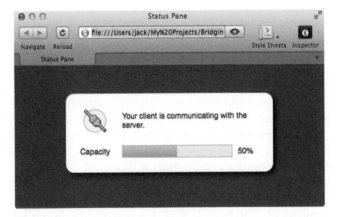

FIGURE 9.9

statusPane_incomplete.html

There's an icon indicating that the client is online and a textual explanation to go with it. Below that is the capacity meter. Everything looks good now, but we need to make sure it behaves properly when there are state changes. We can do that by manually manipulating the classes in the HTML, but this pane is likely to go through a lot of changes in the future, and it will probably have additional readouts added to it. We need a harness that will make testing quick and easy for anyone on your team to do. That's going to take a little bit of extra work now, but it will pay off come version 1.1.

Have a look at the HTML. There are a few things to make note of. First, it looks like there's a state class on the statusPane div:

```
<div class="statusPane online">
```

Hmmm. What would happen if we changed online to be offline? Sure enough, the CSS is already set up to change the display.

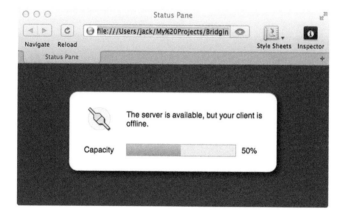

FIGURE 9.10

Offline

Looking further down the DOM, notice that there are actually three messages defined as spans, each one with a class indicating the state that it goes with:

```
<td class="connectionMessage">
    <span class="online">Your client is communicating with the ↵
      server.</span>
    <span class="offline">The server is available, but your ↵
      client is offline.</span>
    <span class="disconnected">Your client is disconnected ↵
      from the server.</span>
</td>
```

"Offline" is going to mean that the client is not currently communicating with the remote server, but that the connection to the server is up. "Disconected" means that the connection is down altogether. Check statusPane.css and you'll find, about half way down, a rule set that hides the spans based on the state class on the statusPane div:

```
.online .offline,
.online .disconnected,
.offline .online,
.offline .disconnected,
.disconnected .online,
.disconnected .offline {
    display: none;
}
```

Just above that are the rules that adjust the background position of the connectionStatus.png sprite:

```
.connection {
    height: 43px;
    width: 43px;
    margin: auto;
    background-image: url(connectionStatus.png);
}

.offline .connection {
    background-position: 0 -43px;
}

.disconnected .connection {
    background-position: 0 -86px;
}
```

With this understanding, we now know that the test harness will have to change that state class. If it can do that, the CSS will handle the rest. Since we have the connection status indicator figured out, let's turn our attention to the capacity meter. The HTML is simple enough:

```
<td class="label">Capacity</td>
<td>
    <div class="barBack">
        <div class="bar gradient"></div>
        <div class="value">50%</div>
    </div>
</td>
```

One div is the background of the meter and contains another div that represents the filled portion. It also contains the numerical readout. The CSS is rather dense, thanks to the gradient being applied to the fill bar:

```
.barBack {
    position: relative;
    height: 20px;
    width: 200px;
    background-color: #dfe9f8;
    border: 1px solid #9cadc6;
}

.bar {
    height: 20px;
    width: 50%;
    background: #c6cede;
    background: -moz-linear-gradient(top, #c6cede 0%, #9eaec7 100%);
    background: -webkit-gradient(linear, left top, left bottom, ⌐
        color-stop(0%,#c6cede), color-stop(100%, #9eaec7));
    background: -webkit-linear-gradient(top, #c6cede 0%,#9eaec7 ⌐
        100%);
    background: -o-linear-gradient(top, #c6cede 0%, #9eaec7 100%);
    background: -ms-linear-gradient(top, #c6cede 0%, #9eaec7 100%);
    background: linear-gradient(to bottom, #c6cede 0%, #9eaec7 100%);
    filter: progid:DXImageTransform.Microsoft.gradient( ⌐
        startColorstr='#c6cede', endColorstr='#9eaec7', ⌐
        GradientType=0 );
}
.value {
    position: absolute;
    top: 2px;
    right: -40px;
}
```

The key thing to note here is that, while the width of .bar is being set to 50%, it's actually going to be set dynamically by JavaScript, as is the percentage value in the HTML. That means the test harness will have to do the same. Let's take stock of what we have to accomplish:

1. Provide a way to switch the connection status state class among three different classes.

2. Provide a means by which to set the width of the fill bar to any percentage.

3. Change the text to display the percentage that the fill bar has been set to.

That doesn't sound too bad. I bet there are some jQuery functions that will make this a snap. First things first, we need to link in the jQuery library. Usually, you'd do this in the ⟨head⟩ of your page. However, since this is just a test harness, we should try to keep it self-contained—make it easy to paste into the page when we need to test and then delete when we're done. To that end, I'm going to set up an area at the end of the document with comments. Do it just above the ⟨/body⟩ tag:

```
<!-- This is a test harness. Remove all code from here to "End of ⌐
    test harness". -->

<!-- End of test harness. -->
```

I've already created the harness.css file with some basic formatting rules for you, so link it in. Then you want to link in the jQuery library as you see here:

```
<!-- This is a test harness. Remove all code from here to "End of ⌐
    test harness". -->
    <link rel="stylesheet" href="harness.css" type="text/css" />
    <script src="jquery-2.1.0.min.js"></script>
<!-- End of test harness. -->
```

Now we should add a couple of UI widgets that will let you change things. I've created a simple framework to hold them that will give some minimal styling through harness.css. Go ahead and add the following HTML:

```
<div class="harnessUI">
    <div class="widgetSet">
    </div>
</div>
```

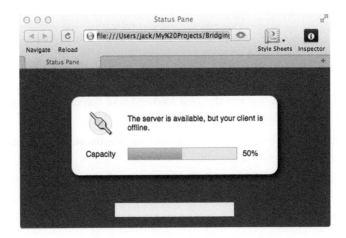

FIGURE 9.11

It's a start.

Now there should be a little, light-gray rectangle centered underneath the status pane. It doesn't have to be pretty, because it's only for your team's use. I've only styled it enough to make it visible and lay out reasonably. So, let's put something in it. Task 1 could be handled by a `<select>` element. We ought to give it a label, and it will need three options: "online", "offline", and "disconnected":

```
<div class="widgetSet"
    <label for="connectionMenu">Client is </label>
    <select class="connectionMenu">
        <option value="online">online</option>
        <option value="offline">offline</option>
        <option value="disconnected">disconnected</option>
    </select>
</div>
```

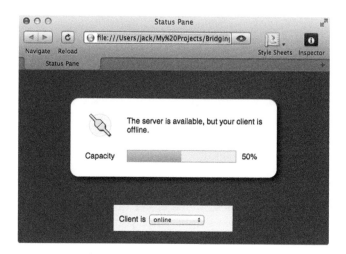

FIGURE 9.12

Connection menu

To enter a percentage value, we just need a field. We'll add it as a second `widgetSet`, and keep the percent sign outside of the field so we don't have to enter it every time we want to change the value. I'm going to go ahead and give it a default value of "50" so that it will match the default specified in the CSS:

```
<div class="widgetSet">
    <label>Capacity <input type="text" class="capacityField" ⏎
        value="50"/> %</label>
</div>
```

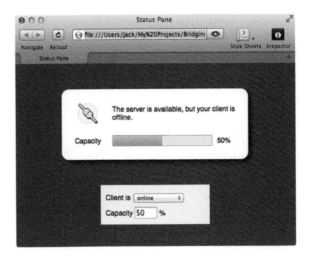

FIGURE 9.13

Capacity field

And with that, we're ready to write some jQuery. There are basically two values we need to manipulate: connection status and capacity. We may as well define those as variables. We can add a `<script>` block directly following the HTML you just entered:

```
<script>
    var connectionStatus;
    var capacity;
</script>
```

One of the reasons jQuery is so much easier to learn than straight JavaScript is that it utilizes CSS syntax. That's right, since you already know CSS, jQuery won't seem completely foreign. We can reference the classes within the HTML to identify the elements we want to find and manipulate. The first thing we need to do is detect a change in the `.connectionMenu`. jQuery has a function for that:

```
$('.connectionMenu').change(function(){ });
```

That dollar sign ($) at the beginning is what calls jQuery. You should recognize the `.connectionMenu` class in the parentheses. In plain English, this line reads, "When connectionMenu changes, do this." The contents of the curly braces (`{ }`) will define what "this" is. We want it to set variable `connectionStatus` to the selection in `.connectionMenu`, so add the following line in the braces:

```
$('.connectionMenu').change(function(){
    connectionStatus=this.value;
});
```

In the new line, `this` is shorthand for the element we identified at the beginning of the script: `.connectionMenu`. Appending `.value` to it indicates that we want the value of `.connectionMenu`. The equal sign (=) means we're assigning that value to your variable, `connectionStatus`. So, the line reads, "Make connectionStatus equal to the value of connectionMenu." As in CSS, the semi-colon (;) marks the end of a line.

Great, we now have a variable containing the value from the menu. All that's left is to insert it as the state class on `.statusPane`. To do that, we'll have to add a new line that identifies `.statusPane`, removes the existing state class, and adds the new one:

```
$('.connectionMenu').change(function(){
    connectionStatus=this.value;
    $('.statusPane').removeClass('online offline ⌐
        disconnected').addClass(connectionStatus);
});
```

The third line starts by selecting `.statusPane`. The `.removeClass` function accepts multiple class names, so we can feed it all three that we know might be there. Finally, `.addClass` uses the variable `connectionStatus`, which is holding the option selected in the menu, which is, conveniently enough, the exact word we need as the new state class. All told, the jQuery statement reads like this: "When connectionMenu changes, set connectionStatus equal to its value. Then remove 'online', 'offline', and 'disconnected' from statusPane, and add the value contained in connectionStatus in their place."

Give it a try. When you select "disconnected", your status pane should look like Figure 9.14.

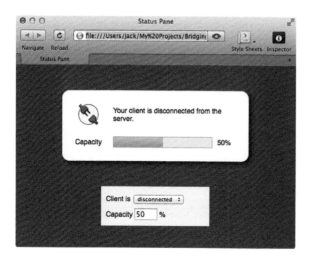

FIGURE 9.14

Disconnected

Alright, let's see to that capacity meter. As with the menu, the first thing we have to do is detect a change in the field. You already know how to do that. Set it up:

```
$('.capacityField').change(function() { });
```

Next, we want to set the `capacity` variable to the value of `.capacityField`. Sound familiar?

```
$('.capacityField').change(function() {
    capacity=this.value;
});
```

All too easy. But here's something different. Rather than swapping classes, we need to set the width of `.bar` to the value now held in `capacity`. We can do that with jQuery's `.width` function:

```
$('.capacityField').change(function() {
    capacity = this.value;
    $('.bar').width(capacity + '%');
});
```

Just as before, we identify the element by the class, `.bar`, and then use `.width` to assign the value held in `capacity`. Since that's only the number, which would be interpreted as pixels, we have to add the percent sign (%). Check it out. As soon as the field loses focus, the fill bar adjusts to the entered percentage.

FIGURE 9.15

Capacity at 80%

Oh, but what about that percentage value to the right of the bar? We can't leave that sitting at 50%. We need one more line of jQuery, this time using the .html function:

```
$('.capacityField').change(function() {
    capacity = $(this).val();
    $('.bar').width(capacity + '%');
    $('.value').html(capacity + '%');
});
```

The last line identifies the .value div and writes its content, replacing anything there with the value in capacity and the added percent sign. If you haven't already, you may as well change the default state class back to online.

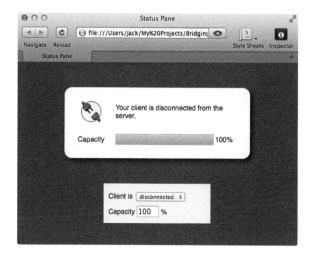

FIGURE 9.16

Uh oh!

Oh, boy. It looks like they're in trouble. They're disconnected and the client server is full. At least we now know that those states all display as they should. But wouldn't it be better if the capacity bar changed color to indicate when it's getting close to full? I bet you could figure out how to do that. I'll leave it in your capable hands.

That was quite a bit to lay on you here in the last chapter. To be honest, it's more than I originally intended to cover, but you see, once I start learning about one thing, it leads me to something else, or more often than not, several somethings. I've discovered new-to-me tools while collecting material for this book, and through the writing, I've deepened my understanding of OOCSS. So, I wanted to not only convince you to improve your HTML and CSS implementation, but to provide you with a number of possible areas for future growth. And how important is all of this to us as designers in the grand scheme of things? Are we starting to get too far afield when we dabble in JavaScript libraries and CSS preprocessors? Is that really part of design? I like Rebekah Cox's perspective:

A good carpenter will know how to use a plane and jigsaw and any number of tools, but that doesn't mean she's not also thinking about what she's building. Rather, she continues to refine her ability to use those tools in order to create the best artifact. Essentially, whatever is created will be the reflection of her skills as a designer of an object, as well as her understanding of her tools.

So, should interface designers be able to build what they design? Probably most can skate by without those skills. Just like someone can do an OK job designing a book or designing a table without really understanding literature or the mechanics of carpentry. But if you want to be a really exceptional designer and really understand how to create something that's the best possible interface that works in the best possible way within the context of digital media, then learning to use the current tools and everything else about that world will only make your understanding and work stronger. Interface design is only about content and construction and design and everything else if you are looking to make something remarkable.

(Part of Rebekah Cox's answer to the question, *"Should user interface designers be able to build what they design?"* on Quora at *http://goo.gl/JdRTVr*.)

Refine your ability to use your tools. Discover tools that you didn't know were available. Make something remarkable. No matter how far you travel, the horizon is always out there in front of you. Never stop learning.

Not the End

How are you doing? Were you able to keep up with my exercises? My workshops have been attended by designers with very basic HTML knowledge, as well as software engineers with much better coding chops than my own. The former had a hard time keeping up with the technical details, but everyone agreed that the vision is compelling and expressed a desire to pursue it. I've followed up with a couple of them who have confirmed that they have been able to start acting upon what they learned, incrementally improving their processes and products. If the code I was asking you to write was a bit beyond you, I encourage you to check out some of the books listed in the References and Resources section. While you're learning more about HTML and CSS, keep this book handy. Revisit the later chapters as they become more relevant to you. Hopefully, they'll keep you from making the same mistakes I made. If, on the other hand, everything I've told you is old hat, please pass my book along to someone who you think will benefit from it.

For everyone else, I offer a challenge. Embrace your inner unicorn. Don't allow your research, expertise, and creativity to be marginalized by inferior craftsmanship and a lack of attention to detail. Don't just work with your developers; become an integral part of the team. And please, let me know how it goes. Just as I enjoy hearing about the careers of my former students, it'd be gratifying to know how this book has helped you. Of course, as any good designer should be, I'm interested in hearing criticism as well. Feel free to contact me any time by email (jackmoffett@mac.com) or on Twitter (@jackmoffett).

Whatever you do, don't stop here. There's so much more to learn. This is the end of a book, but it's just another stepping stone in your journey.

References and Resources

This appendix provides links to all of the articles, books, and tools I referenced throughout the book, as well as some that I didn't reference but think you should know about. You're welcome!

HOW TO FIND ME

DesignAday: *http://designaday.tumblr.com*
Twitter: *https://twitter.com/jackmoffett*
LinkedIn: *http://goo.gl/q1BJH5*
Speaker Deck: *https://speakerdeck.com/jackmoffett*
Facebook: *https://www.facebook.com/jacklmoffett*

SURVEY

Survs—the web service I used to create and conduct the survey discussed in Chapter 1: *http://www.survs.com*

Survey Results on GitHub: *http://git.io/G7WfzQ*

Language Proficiency of Interaction Designers on Many Eyes: *http://goo.gl/PkyZsh*

Interaction Design Association (IxDA): *http://www.ixda.org*

IxDA LinkedIn group: *http://goo.gl/6oVycJ*

Parallel set visualizations were created using Parallel Sets, an application created by Robert Kosara and Caroline Ziemkiewicz: *http://eagereyes.org/parallel-sets*

DESIGNERS WORKING WITH DEVELOPERS

Working with Developers on DesignAday: *http://goo.gl/mUyhwo*

How Designers and Engineers Can Play Nice (and Still Run with Scissors), Jenna Bilotta: *http://goo.gl/XI6SEL*

How to Partner and Work with a Designer, interview with Uday Gajendar: *http://youtu.be/aS5vIXbRvOU*

Partnering with a UI Designer, Uday Gajendar: *http://goo.gl/GnnwGy*

Three's Company: A Proven Model for Good Development, Uday Gajendar: *http://goo.gl/ZpGgAR*

Ghost in the Pixel, blog by Uday Gajendar: *http://www.ghostinthepixel.com*

LEARNING TO CODE

Learning to Code on DesignAday: *http://goo.gl/PA5ulY*

Do Designers Need to Be Able to Code?, discussion on IxDA LinkedIn group: *http://goo.gl/Y3XdVi*

Why the Valley Wants Designers That Can Code, Jared Spool: *http://www.uie.com/brainsparks/?p=4358*

Unicorn, Shmunicorn—Be a Pegasus, Wayne Greenwood: *http://www.waynegreenwood.com/?p=562*

"Designers Shouldn't Code" Is the Wrong Answer to the Right Question, Joshua Seiden: *http://wp.me/pYa2H-4J*

Thoughts on Code, Programming, Design, Production, Development, Technology, and Oh! Design, Dave Malouf: *http://davemalouf.com/?p=2390*

Design, Production, and Craft: What Do Designers Make?, Matt Nish-Lapidus: *http://ideas.normative.com/?p=1007*

Designers That Code: A Response to Jared Spool, Jennifer Tidwell: *http://designinginterfaces.com/?p=392*

On Being T-Shaped, Tim Brown: *http://goo.gl/pZoy83*

Coding for Designers, Matt Nish-Lapidus: *http://ideas.normative.com/?p=373*

Quora: Should user interface designers be able to build what they design?: *http://goo.gl/JdRTVr*

Unicorn Institute: *http://unicorninstitute.com*

INTERESTING MOMENTS GRID

Designing for Interesting Moments, slide deck by Bill Scott: *http://goo.gl/NugG6C*

Capturing the Interesting Moments, Jared Spool: *http://goo.gl/Wq7GyV*

HTML AND CSS

CSS 3 for Web Designers, Dan Cederholm: *http://goo.gl/f6sxQk*

HTML5 for Web Designers, Jeremy Keith: *http://goo.gl/IVZtFp*

Sass for Web Designers, Dan Cederholm: *http://goo.gl/MXdLSe*

Responsive Web Design, Ethan Marcotte: *http://goo.gl/3EDLO9*

Thinking with Type, Ellen Lupton: *http://www.thinkingwithtype.com*

Principles of Writing Consistent, Idiomatic CSS, Nicolas Gallagher: *http://git.io/qS6zjA*

CSS Sprites: Image Slicing's Kiss of Death, Dave Shea: *http://goo.gl/YwISfG*

OOCSS

Nicole Sullivan: *http://www.stubbornella.org*

OOCSS: *https://github.com/stubbornella/oocss/wiki*

Brian Cavalier: *http://www.briancavalier.com*

OOCSS for JavaScript Pirates: *http://goo.gl/kdrpz4*

cujoJS: *http://cujojs.com*

An Introduction to Object Oriented CSS (OOCSS), Louis Lazaris: *http://coding.smashingmagazine.com/?p=116652*

Scalable and Modular Architecture for CSS (SMACSS), Jonathan Snook: *http://smacss.com*

Bridging UX and Web Development on GitHub: *http://git.io/28dKkg*

TOOLBOX

Tool	Developer	Platform	URL
BBEdit	Bare Bones Software	Mac	*www.barebones.com*
Bootstrap	Bootstrap core team		*http://getbootstrap.com*
Brackets	Adobe/Open Source	Mac, Windows, Linux	*www.brackets.io*
Chrome	Google	Mac, Windows, Linux	*www.google.com*
Coda	Panic	Mac	*www.panic.com*

Tool	Developer	Platform	URL
Codebase	aTech Media	Web	www.codebasehq.com
CodeKit	Bryan Jones	Mac	https://incident57.com/codekit/
Confluence	Atlassian	Web	www.atlassian.com
Cornerstone	Zennaware	Mac	www.zennaware.com
CSS Lint	Nicholas C. Zakas and Nicole Sullivan	Web	http://csslint.net/
Dojo	The Dojo Foundation		http://dojotoolkit.org
Dreamweaver	Adobe	Mac, Windows	www.adobe.com
Emmet	Sergey Chikuyonok		www.emmet.io
Espresso	MacRabbit	Mac	www.macrabbit.com
FileMerge	Apple	Mac	www.developer.apple.com
Firefox and Firebug	Mozilla	Mac, Windows, Linux	www.getfirebug.com
FishEye	Atlassian	Web	www.atlassian.com
Git	Open Source	Mac, Windows, Linux, Solaris	www.git-scm.com
Gitbox	Oleg Andreev	Mac	www.gitboxapp.com
GitHub	GitHub	Mac, Windows, Linux	www.github.com
Hammer	Riot	Mac	http://hammerformac.com
Internet Explorer	Microsoft	Windows	www.microsoft.com
JIRA	Atlassian	Web	www.atlassian.com
jQuery	The jQuery Foundation		http://jquery.com
Kaleidoscope	Black Pixel	Mac	www.blackpixel.com
Koala	Ethan Lai	Mac, Windows, Linux	http://koala-app.com
Less	Less core team		http://lesscss.org
LiveReload	Andrey Tarantsov	Mac	http://livereload.com/
Macaw	Macaw	Mac	www.macaw.co
Mercurial	Open Source	Mac, Windows, Linux, Solaris	www.mercurial.selenic.com
Modernizr	Modernizr team		http://modernizr.com
MooTools	MooTools Dev Team		http://mootools.net
ProCSSor	HyperText Assembly	Web, Mac	www.procssor.com

Tool	Developer	Platform	URL
Prototype	Prototype Core Team		*http://prototypejs.org*
Remote Desktop Connection	Microsoft	Mac, Windows	*www.microsoft.com*
Safari	Apple	Mac, Windows	*www.apple.com*
Sass	Team Sass		*http://sass-lang.com*
Scout	Mutually Human	Mac, Windows	*http://mhs.github.io/scout-app/*
Selectivizr	Keith Clark		*http://selectivizr.com*
SimpLESS	KISS	Mac, Windows	*http://wearekiss.com/simpless*
SourceTree	Atlassian	Mac, Windows	*www.sourcetreeapp.com*
Stylus	LearnBoost		*http://learnboost.github.io/stylus/*
Sublime Text	Sublime HQ	Mac, Windows, Linux	*www.sublimetext.com*
Subversion	Apache	Mac, Windows, Unix, BeOS, OS/2	*www.subversion.apache.org*
TextMate	MacroMates	Mac	*www.macromates.com*
TextWrangler	Bare Bones Software	Mac	*www.barebones.com*
TopStyle	TopStyle	Windows	*www.topstyle4.com*
TortoiseSVN	Open Source	Windows	*www.tortoisesvn.net*
Tower	Fournova	Mac	*www.git-tower.com*
Trello	Fog Creek Software	Web, iOS, Android	*www.trello.com*
Versions	Black Pixel	Mac	*www.blackpixel.com*
WebStorm	JetBrains	Mac, Windows, Linux	*http://www.jetbrains.com/webstorm/*
YUI	Yahoo		*http://yuilibrary.com*

Glossary

Acronym	Term	Definition
	Agile	Agile software development is a group of software development methods based on iterative and incremental development, where requirements and solutions evolve through collaboration between self-organizing, cross-functional teams. *http://en.wikipedia.org/wiki/Agile_software_development*
	Argument	In mathematics and computer programming, an argument is an independent variable that is provided as an input to a function. In this way, the function may be written without knowing what values will be calculated. *http://en.wikipedia.org/wiki/Independent_variables*
	Attribute	In HTML, attributes provide additional information about an element. They're specified in the start tag and are composed of name–value pairs, such as `id="myDiv"`.
	Baseline	Refers to a software release, as tracked by a version control system. Also referred to as a *tag* or *label*.
	Blame	A feature within a version control system that displays the name of the developer who last touched each line of code in a version of a file.
	Burndown Chart	A graphical representation of work left to do versus time.
	Branch	Refers to a version of a software product maintained in parallel with the main version (the trunk), as tracked by a version control system. As a verb, it's the act of creating a branch. Also referred to as a *fork*.

Acronym	Term	Definition
	C++	One of the most popular programming languages. Used for writing software of all kinds on a variety of operating systems and platforms. It must be compiled to run. *http://en.wikipedia.org/wiki/C%2B%2B*
	Class	In HTML, it's an attribute that specifies one or more class names. Class names correspond to selectors in a CSS file.
	Commit	The act of checking changes into a version control system. As a noun, it can also refer to the set of files that were checked in.
CMS	Content Management System	A computer program that allows publishing, editing, and modifying content, as well as maintenance, from a central interface. *http://en.wikipedia.org/wiki/Content_management_system*
	Critical Path	The longest sequence of necessary tasks that must be completed in a project, respecting their interdependencies. If you're on the critical path during implementation, you have the potential to create bottlenecks for the team.
.ear	Enterprise Archive	A file format used by Java EE for packaging one or more modules into a single archive so that the deployment of the various modules onto an application server happens simultaneously and coherently. *http://en.wikipedia.org/wiki/EAR_(file_format)*
	Fork	Refers to a version of a software product maintained in parallel with the main version (the trunk), as tracked by a version control system. As a verb, it's the act of creating a fork. Also referred to as a *branch*.
DFD	Data Flow Diagram	A graphical representation of the "flow" of data through an information system, modeling its process aspects. A DFD shows what kinds of information will be input to and output from the system, where the data will come from and go to, and where the data will be stored. *http://en.wikipedia.org/wiki/Data_flow_diagram*
	Declaration	In CSS, a declaration is part of a CSS rule. It's composed of a property (e.g., color) and a value (e.g., blue). One or more declarations specify the structure and skin attributes of an HTML element.
	Declaration Block	The part of a CSS rule containing declarations.
	Descendant Selector	A descendant selector matches all elements that are descendants of its ancestor element. For example, in the selector `div span`, `span` is the descendant selector and will target every span in a page that's a descendant of a div.
	Diff	Refers to the act of checking for differences between files. It may be used as a noun or a verb. You can "run a diff," and you can "diff a file."

Acronym	Term	Definition
DOM	Document Object Model	A cross-platform and language-independent convention for representing and interacting with objects in HTML, XHTML, and XML documents. Objects in the DOM tree may be addressed and manipulated by using methods on the objects. *http://en.wikipedia.org/wiki/Document_Object_Model*
	DOM Manipulation	Using JavaScript to make changes in a web page by adding, removing, or changing HTML elements.
	Element	The primitive objects that make up an HTML page. A typical element is composed of content surrounded by opening and closing tags. The opening tag may contain attributes (e.g., `<p class="sampleText">This is sample text.</p>`).
	Embedded CSS	Any CSS rules that are written into an HTML page, rather than being relegated to an external style sheet. CSS can be embedded in the header or inline as an attribute.
	Engineering Prototype	A piece of software written to test a technical theory or a technology. They're used early in a project's schedule so that developers can determine strategies for implementation.
	Extend	In CSS extension languages, an extend copies the rules from one ruleset into another rule set. The rule set that receives the extend is then an extension of the first ruleset.
	Framework	A universal, reusable software platform that includes support programs, compilers, code libraries, tool sets, and application programming interfaces (APIs). *http://en.wikipedia.org/wiki/Software_framework*
	Function	In JavaScript, a block of code that's executed when another piece of code calls it. This is referred to generically in computer programming as a subroutine. *http://en.wikipedia.org/wiki/Function_(computer_science)*
FRD	Functional Requirements Document	Contractual document specifying the functionality that a software application must exhibit to meet the needs of a customer.
	Functional Testing	Functional testing verifies that each function within a software application does what the design document, FRD, or other specifications state that it should.
	Gantt Chart	A type of bar chart illustrating the start and finish dates of a project's tasks. It depicts dependencies between tasks and may indicate the percent completion of each task.
GWT	Google Web Toolkit	A development toolkit for building and optimizing complex, browser-based applications. *http://www.gwtproject.org*

Acronym	Term	Definition
GUI	Graphical User Interface	Allows people to interact with a computer through intuitive, visual representations of functionality, rather than by typing obscure commands. But you knew that, didn't you?
	Head	The most recent version of a codebase, as tracked by a version control system. May also be referred to as the *tip*.
	Identity Class	In OOCSS, the identity (or identifier) class defines the default state of an element.
	Inline CSS	CSS written into an HTML page as a style attribute on an element.
IDE	Integrated Development Environment	A software application that provides comprehensive facilities to computer programmers for software development. An IDE normally consists of a source code editor, build automation tools, and a debugger. Most modern IDEs offer intelligent code completion features. *http://en.wikipedia.org/wiki/Integrated_development_environment*
	Issue Tracking	In software development, software is used to organize tasks, bugs, improvements, and other issues. There's typically a workflow, allowing issues to be assigned to people, attributed state, and eventually resolved.
JAXP	Java API for XML Processing	Provides the capability of validating and parsing XML documents. *http://en.wikipedia.org/wiki/JAXP*
	jQuery	jQuery is a fast, small, and feature-rich JavaScript library. It makes things like HTML document traversal and manipulation, event handling, animation, and Ajax much simpler with an easy-to-use API that works across a multitude of browsers. *http://jquery.com*
JSP	JavaServer Pages	A technology that helps software developers create dynamically generated web pages based on HTML, XML, or other document types. It's similar to PHP, but it uses the Java programming language. *http://en.wikipedia.org/wiki/JavaServer_Pages*
	Label	Refers to a software release, as tracked by a version control system. Also referred to as a *baseline* or *tag*.
	Lean UX	Inspired by Lean and Agile development theories, Lean UX is the practice of bringing the true nature of our work to light faster, with less emphasis on deliverables and greater focus on the actual experience being designed. *http://uxdesign.smashingmagazine.com/2011/03/07/lean-ux-getting-out-of-the-deliverables-business/*

Acronym	Term	Definition
Less	Leaner CSS	A CSS extension language, also referred to as a preprocessor. It is also the file extension for its file type (.less). *http://lesscss.org*
	Long Pole in the Tent	The pole that holds the most weight. In a project, the person with the most work assigned to them is considered "the long pole in the tent."
	Mixin	In object-oriented programming languages, a mixin is a class that contains a combination of methods from other classes. In CSS extension languages, mixins reference multiple rules, allowing them to be reused in multiple rule sets. *http://en.wikipedia.org/wiki/Mixin*
MRD	Marketing Requirements Document	This document is typically written by product marketing or product management. The intent is to express the customer's wants or needs for a product.
	Merge	The act of combining multiple versions of a file (or set of files) that have had changes made. May also be used as a noun to refer to the process of merging.
	Merge Conflict	When two versions of a document are merged, a merge conflict will occur when changes have been made to the same content (e.g., line of code) in both files. Such a conflict must be resolved by a person.
	Modifier Class	In OOCSS, a modifier class is used to apply changes to an identity, or base, class. For example, in the attribute `class="footerBar mini"`, the `footerBar` class establishes the default styling of the element, while `mini` modifies it with additional styling or overrides.
	Namespace	In OOCSS, a namespace is created by assigning a class to an ancestral element. This class name may then be used in selectors to treat other classes differently than they would be outside of the namespace.
	.NET	A software framework developed by Microsoft that runs primarily on Windows. *http://en.wikipedia.org/wiki/.NET*
	Object	In OOCSS, an object is basically any HTML element.
OOCSS	Object-oriented CSS	An approach to writing CSS that encourages code reuse and results in more efficient and more easily maintained style sheets.
PHP	PHP: Hypertext Preprocessor	A server-side scripting language designed for web development. *http://en.wikipedia.org/wiki/PHP*
	Pseudo-class, Pseudo-selector	In CSS, they're used to create behavior for special states of elements, such as when the cursor hovers over an element.
	Pseudo-state	One of the states targeted by a pseudo-class.

Acronym	Term	Definition
Regex	Regular Expression	A sequence of characters that forms a search pattern. *http://en.wikipedia.org/wiki/Regular_expression*
	Regression Test	A type of software testing that seeks to uncover new software bugs, or regressions, in existing functional and nonfunctional areas of a system after changes, such as enhancements, patches, or configuration changes, have been made to them. *http://en.wikipedia.org/wiki/Regression_testing*
	Repository	The container for your software codebase. It's maintained by a version control system on a server. It's that which you check files out of and commit changes to.
	Ruby on Rails	An open-source web application framework. *http://en.wikipedia.org/wiki/Ruby_on_Rails*
	Rule, Rule Set	In CSS, a rule or rule set is comprised of one or more selectors followed by one or more declarations.
Sass	Syntactically Awesome Style Sheets	A CSS extension language, also referred to as a preprocessor. In all caps (SASS), or as a file extension (.sass), it refers to Sass's original syntax and file type. *http://sass-lang.com*
SCSS	Sassy CSS	Sass's newer syntax, which includes standard CSS syntax. It's also the extension for its file type (.scss).
	Selector	In CSS, the part of a rule that targets an HTML element or group of elements. A selector is a pattern composed of element types, IDs, classes, pseudo-states, etc.
	Skin	In OOCSS, skin refers to the nonstructural attributes of an HTML element (e.g., color, font style, background image).
	State Change Diagram	Depicts the various states that a system can be in and the actions and conditions that result in those states.
	State Class	In OOCSS, a state class is added to an element to change its appearance in the HTML page when a particular state is in effect.
	Structure	In OOCSS, structure refers to attributes that affect an element's position, size, or shape (e.g., height, left, float).
	Stylus	A CSS extension language, also referred to as a preprocessor. *http://learnboost.github.io/stylus/*
	Tag	Refers to a software release, as tracked by a version control system. Also referred to as a *baseline* or *label*.
	Task Management	Software development teams use software to assign tasks, estimate effort, and track completion.

Acronym	Term	Definition
	Technology Stack	The layers of components and services used to create software.
	Tip	The most recent version of a codebase, as tracked by a version control system. May also be referred to as the *head*.
	Trunk	The main version of a codebase, as tracked by a version control system.
UML	Unified Modeling Language	Combines techniques from data modeling (entity relationship diagrams), business modeling (workflows), object modeling, and component modeling. It can be used with all processes, throughout the software development life cycle, and across different implementation technologies. *http://en.wikipedia.org/wiki/Unified_Modeling_Language*
	Variable	In computer programming, a variable is a symbolic name that values can be assigned to and retrieved from. *http://en.wikipedia.org/wiki/Variable_(computer_science)*
VCS	Version Control System	A software application used for managing versions of a software application, as well as versions of its individual files. *http://en.wikipedia.org/wiki/Revision_control*
VM	Virtual Machine	A software implementation of a physical computer. A server can host multiple VMs, which developers can connect to and run applications on over the network. This is more efficient and cost effective than standing up physical machines for every instance needed by a development team.
W3C	World Wide Web Consortium	The main international standards organization for the World Wide Web. *http://www.w3.org*
	Working Copy	The local copy of a codebase checked out of a version control system. A developer makes changes to the code in the working copy. When the changes are complete and tested, the developer checks them in.
WYSIWYG	What You See Is What You Get	Refers to software user interfaces that allow you to edit content in a view that mimics the final output.
XML	Extensible Markup Language	Defines a set of rules for encoding documents in a format that's both human-readable and machine-readable. *http://en.wikipedia.org/wiki/XML*
XSLT	Extensible Stylesheet Language Transformations	A language for transforming XML documents into other XML documents or other objects, such as HTML for web pages, plain text, or XSL formatting objects, which can then be converted to PDF, PostScript, and PNG. *http://en.wikipedia.org/wiki/XSLT*

Index

Related Titles from Morgan Kaufmann

User Experience Management
Essential Skills for Leading Effective UX Teams
Arnie Lund
9780123854964

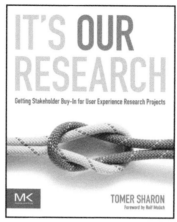

It's Our Research
Getting Stakeholder Buy-In for
User Experience Research Projects
Tomer Sharon
9780123851307

Quantifying the User Experience
Practical Statistics for User Research
Jeff Sauro and James R. Lewis
9780123849687

Measuring the User Experience
Collecting, Analyzing, and Presenting
Usability Metrics
Tom Tullis and Bill Albert
9780123735584

Letting Go of the Words,
Second Edition
Writing Web Content that Works
Janice (Ginny) Redish
9780123859303

Designing with the Mind in Mind,
Second Edition
Simple Guide to Understanding User Interface
Design Guidelines
Jeff Johnson
9780124079144

mkp.com

Related Titles from Morgan Kaufmann

Printed and bound by CPI Group (UK) Ltd, Croydon, CR0 4YY

08/06/2025

01896869-0014